S. P. Doughty

Willie Benton

Or, the Soldier's Boy and other Stories

S. P. Doughty

Willie Benton
Or, the Soldier's Boy and other Stories

ISBN/EAN: 9783337129880

Printed in Europe, USA, Canada, Australia, Japan

Cover: Foto ©ninafisch / pixelio.de

More available books at **www.hansebooks.com**

WILLIE BENTON

OR, THE SOLDIER'S BOY

AND

OTHER STORIES

By MRS. S. P. DOUGHTY

AUTHOR OF
"PLAYING SANTA CLAUS AND OTHER TALES" AND "STORIES
AND RHYMES FOR BOYS AND GIRLS"

BOSTON
HENRY H. & T. W. CARTER
1869

Entered according to Act of Congress, in the
HENRY H. & T. W. CARTER,
In the Clerk's office of the District Court of the D

STEREOTYPED BY INNES, REGAN & LEASURE
55 Water Street, Boston.

Presswork by Henry H. & T. W. Carter.

CONTENTS.

	Page
WILLIE BENTON; OR, THE SOLDIER'S BOY . . .	5
SIXTY MINUTES MAKE ONE HOUR	34
THE LOST KNIFE; OR, BEARING FALSE WITNESS.	59
MAKING THE BEST OF IT	72
ISABEL'S BIRTHDAY	88
"I'LL TELL MOTHER"	110
THE CHRISTMAS GIFTS	116
GOING DOWN HILL	127
CLARA'S BIRTHDAY; OR, THE MOTIVE MAKES THE DEED	139
OUR WORK	144
HENRY'S NAP IN THE ARBOR	164
MISCHIEVOUS TOM; OR, IT IS ONLY FOR FUN . .	177

WILLIE BENTON;
OR,
THE SOLDIER'S BOY.

WILLIE BENTON was a very happy little boy. He lived in a pleasant cottage, far away among the hills and mountains, in one of the Eastern States, with his father and mother, who loved him very dearly. Mr. Benton was a laboring man, and supported his little family by working for the wealthy farmers in the neighborhood.

He was industrious and faithful, and an excellent workman, and could always obtain steady employment. He was also an intelligent man, and had received a tolerably good common school education when he was young, which he now found to be a great blessing to him.

When his day's work was done, he would often

spend an hour in working about his own home, and when his supper was over, and he had played with little Willie until his mother was ready to put him into his trundle-bed, he would take some interesting and instructive book, and read aloud for an hour or two, while his wife was busy with her needle.

Willie liked to look at pictures, and hear little stories, very much; and when he was three years old his father brought him home a primer, and a slate and pencil, for he said it was time to begin to teach Willie his letters, and that he should show them to him in the book, and then make them on the slate to help him to remember their form. Willie was very much pleased with the primer, but he was still more delighted with the slate and pencil. He had never seen one before, and he thought it the most wonderful thing in the world. When his father made two or three letters on the slate for him to look at, he clapped his hands joyfully, and wanted to take the pencil himself, and try if he could not make some too. His father gave him the pencil, and was quite astonished to find that Willie could make letters very nearly as well as he could. The little boy was quite proud of his success, and after making several letters, he suddenly exclaimed, —

"Now I will make mother!" and he immediately drew the figure of a woman, which, though it did not bear much resemblance to his mother, was so well drawn that Mr. Benton hastily called his wife from the next room to come and look at it, and told her in a whisper that he really believed the boy would make an artist, for he could already draw much better than he could do.

Mrs. Benton smiled, and said that she used to draw pretty well when she was a young girl, and then she looked at Willie's letters, and at the picture of herself, and seemed very much pleased.

From this time, Willie's slate and pencil were his constant companions. Almost everything that he saw he would try to draw upon his slate. He made pictures of horses and cows, and dogs and cats, and sheep and lambs, and houses, and trees, and men and women, and children. Of course, they were only rough sketches, but they were really wonderfully well done for such a little child.

But Willie's happy days were not to last very long. The war had commenced, and though for some time Mr. Benton did not think it his duty to leave his wife and child, yet, as the call for men became more urgent, he at length yielded, and after making every arrangement for their comfort, he bade them a sorrowful farewell, and joined the troops who were about marching from his native State.

This was a great trial to Mrs. Benton, but she looked to the Lord for strength, and tried hard to do her duty.

During the first year of her husband's absence she heard from him frequently, and as he seemed in good health and spirits, she gradually recovered her cheerfulness, and looked forward with hope to the time of his return. She took great pains with Willie's reading, and he learned rapidly, although he did not enjoy it so much as drawing on his darling slate. His mother often gave him a little piece of paper and a lead pencil, that he might draw some little picture to send to his father, or write him a little letter, and Willie could print the letters so neatly, and put the words together so well, that he could really make out a very neat little letter. And then his father would send him one in return, telling him how much he loved him and thought of him, and how happy it made him to receive his little note, and the pretty pictures which he sometimes sent.

But at length there came news of a fearful battle, in which the regiment to which Mr. Benton belonged was actively engaged; and as the days passed on, and not a line was received to tell of his safety, his poor wife's heart grew very sad, and her anxiety became so great that she found it almost impossible to attend to her daily duties. At last the list of the killed and wounded appeared in the daily papers, and the cause of his silence was now explained, for the name of William Benton was the first among the many who had fallen in his company.

Willie watched his mother as the paper fell from her hand, and she sunk back in the chair so white and motionless, and although he was too young to understand the meaning of what he saw, he was much alarmed, and running to her side, begged her to speak to him, and tell him what was the matter. But as all his efforts to make her speak were in vain, he brought his little cricket and seated himself at her feet, and leaning his head upon her lap, sobbed aloud. A kind neighbor, who had heard the sad news, soon came in, and she laid Mrs. Benton upon the bed, and after a while succeeded in restoring her to consciousness. But she had always been a feeble woman, and this great shock, added to the anxiety which she had endured for many days, was too much for her strength, and for weeks she was too ill to leave her bed, or to attend to the wants of her little Willie. The good woman who had first come to her assistance was her only near neighbor, and she was a widow, with a family of children to attend to. Of course she had but little time to spare, but when she could not go herself to help her poor neighbor, she would send her little girls, who, though not more than eight or ten years old, were bright, handy little things, and tried to do their very best; and after a few days, those who had employed Mr. Benton before he became a soldier heard of the situation of his wife, and sent or came to see if they could do anything for her relief.

It was early spring when she was taken ill, and the roses were in bloom before she was again able to perform her usual duties. Willie thought himself a very happy boy when his dear mother could sit up and walk about the rooms once more. He had wept bitterly when first told of his father's death, but his tears were soon dried, for he had learned to live without him, and did not really miss him as he missed his mother, when she was too ill to attend to him. Mrs. Benton gradually grew more resigned and cheerful, and tried to forget her own grief in earnest endeavors to do all she could for the little one who was now left to her sole charge.

The gentleman who owned her little cottage was one for whom her husband had often worked, and who had always been very friendly toward them. He had called to see Mrs. Benton, and had kindly told her that she was quite welcome to continue to live in the cottage, rent free, as long as she pleased.

"When my little friend Willie is old enough to help you, it will be time enough to talk about rent," he said.

Mrs. Benton thanked him most gratefully for his kindness. She still had a little money laid by, but it was only a little, and she wished to make it last as long as possible, until her health and strength should fully return, and she should be able to think of some way in which she could provide for herself and Willie.

But health and strength did not return. During

the pleasant summer weather she was able to work a little in the cottage, and sometimes even took a short walk with Willie, or helped him in his little garden; but when the autumn came, she grew more feeble, and had a distressing cough, which troubled her very much, both night and day. Winter set in early, and the snow was soon very deep. Mrs. Benton lived in a lonely place; and now that the weather was so severe, and the roads difficult to travel, she seldom saw any one excepting her good neighbor Mrs. Allen, and her children. They were always kind and thoughtful, and when the morning was cold and stormy, the eldest boy, George, would always knock at her door at an early hour, and say that he had come to do what he could to make her comfortable before he went to his work; for George was eleven years old; and as his mother was a poor widow with several other children to support, she could not afford to send him to school when he could find any employment by which he could earn even a little to help along.

Mrs. Benton would smile and thank him very gratefully, as he brought her wood and water for the day; and little Willie would often say,—

"You are a good boy, George, and I will draw you the very prettiest picture I can."

Then George would go whistling to his work, with his heart warmed and made glad by the thought that he had done a kind action.

Every day, and sometimes two or three times in the day, would good Mrs. Allen bustle in, and, in her cheerful way, say she had a few minutes to spare, and had come to do some "little turn" for her sick neighbor. She was not a woman of as much education or refinement as Mrs. Benton, but her heart was full of kindness, and she would willingly have denied herself many comforts for the sake of helping the widow and her orphan boy.

Mrs. Benton was cheered and comforted by these acts of kindness, and endeavored to make some return by teaching her kind neighbor's children to read and write, and sometimes giving George a little instruction in arithmetic, in the long evenings, after Willie was asleep.

She often suffered much pain, and had days of great weakness, but she hoped and believed that when the mild weather returned, she should gain strength, and that her cough and other troubles would pass away.

But this was not to be. Death came very suddenly at last. For several days she had seemed uncommonly well, and Willie had rejoiced that dear mamma was growing so strong, and did not cough so hard any more. Then came a sudden change; and, before the frightened child could bring Mrs. Allen to her aid, she was quite unable to speak, and could only look imploringly at her kind friend, and then turn her eyes toward her darling boy.

"He shall never want a friend," said the good woman, as she vainly strove, by rubbing and other means, to restore animation to the almost lifeless form. But all her efforts were useless, and in a few moments the spirit passed peacefully away.

Weeks passed: Willie had been taken to Mrs. Allen's house, and the furniture at the cottage had been sold; and what little money remained after the funeral expenses were defrayed, had been given to her for his benefit. It was but a small sum, however, and the poor woman felt that it would be no easy thing for her to bear this additional burden. But she remembered her promises to his dying mother, and she could not bear the thought of giving him up to the town. "I will do all I can for the poor little fellow," she said, "and perhaps the Lord will show me the way to provide for him."

Willie grieved sadly for his mother; and although all were kind to him, he was not happy in his new home. He had always lived alone with his mother, or with his father and mother, and it seemed strange to him to be with so many children. And then good Mrs. Allen was not at all like his own gentle mother. Willie, therefore, felt lonely and homesick, and instead of being the merry little fellow he once had been, grew so quiet and sad that Mrs. Allen feared he was ill.

"Poor thing," she would sometimes say with a sigh, "he is just wearing away like his poor mother. I do not think he has long to stay in this world."

But Willie was not really ill, although he looked rather pale and thin, and did not frolic and play with the other children, but would sit for hours busy with his slate and pencil, or reading in the little Bible from which his mother had so often read aloud to him.

One day, about the middle of the summer, while the children were playing near the cottage, and

Mrs. Allen was busy in her little kitchen, a travelling carriage was seen slowly winding its way up a steep hill at a little distance. As it came nearly opposite the cottage, the driver reined up his horses, and beckoning to one of the older children, inquired which was the shortest road to a neighboring town. The child not knowing how to reply, ran to call her mother, and Mrs. Allen soon appeared at the door, wiping her hands upon her apron, and dropping a curtsey as she advanced toward the carriage.

"The right-hand road is the most travelled," she said to the driver, "and it will lead you to the centre of the town."

"Thank you, my good woman," replied a very pleasant looking gentleman, leaning out of the carriage window. "Can you oblige us by giving this lady a glass of water?" and as he spoke he looked toward a gentle, delicate-looking lady by his side, who also leaned forward, and smiling kindly upon Mrs. Allen, seemed to gaze with much interest upon the group of children who stood eagerly watching the strangers.

The water was quickly brought, and as the lady handed back the glass, she said, —

"You have a fine family of children, my friend. Are these all yours?"

"Yes ma'am, I may say they are all mine,—all but the little fellow seated on the rock yonder, with the slate and pencil in his hand; he is a stray lamb, poor thing. His father was killed in the war, and his mother died not many months ago, with a broken heart, I am thinking."

"Poor child!" exclaimed the lady, with much interest; "and were you a near relative of the father or mother?"

"Not a bit of a relative, ma'am, only a neighbor. We lived in a kind of a lonely way here, and, of course, I did all I could for her, and at last, when she died kind of sudden like, I promised to be a friend to the child; so he shares with my own, ma'am, which is all I can do."

"Certainly it is," replied the gentleman, who was also listening to the story with much interest; "but has the child no near relations?"

"Not one, sir; I have often heard the poor mother say that there was no one to claim kindred with her, or with the father either."

"It must be quite a charge for you, in addition

to your own family, my good woman. Is your husband living?"

"No, sir; I have been a widow these four years. The poor orphan is welcome to all we can do for him, but he feels lonely and strange-like among us. His father and mother were different from what we are, sir, quite different indeed;—poor enough, to be sure, but they had a deal of learning, and the mother was a born lady."

"Cannot we get out of the carriage for awhile, and rest in this pleasant place?" asked the lady of her husband. "I should so love to talk to the little boy, and to see all the children."

The gentleman looked at his watch, and replied that an hour's delay would be of no consequence, and directed the coachman to drive to a shady place, and let the horses rest a little.

Mrs. Allen kindly invited the gentleman and lady to enter the cottage, but they preferred remaining outside with the children, and begged the good woman to return to her work, promising to come in and see her before they left.

The lady then seated herself upon a rock very near to where Willie was still sitting, with his slate and pencil in his hand, although he had stopped drawing, and was looking earnestly at the lady. She smiled upon him, and said, —

"You have a pretty little slate. Have you been drawing a picture?"

"Yes, ma'am," replied Willie, timidly.

"And will you show it to me?" asked the lady, holding out her hand as she spoke.

Willie rose and brought her the slate. There was a picture of a lady sitting in a chair with a book in her hand, and a little boy seated at her feet. It was, of course, very imperfectly drawn, but still it seemed a remarkable drawing for so young a child, and the lady exclaimed with surprise, —

"Did you draw this all yourself, my little boy?"

"Yes, ma'am," replied Willie. "It is a picture of my mother and me. This is my mother," he continued, pointing to the figure on the slate; "she is reading the Bible aloud, and this is me sitting at her feet and listening to her. Only the face is not much like my mother's. I cannot make it quite right. She looked like you, I think, ma'am."

"Did she indeed?" replied the lady, smiling. "Then I suppose you will love me a little, will you not?"

"Yes, ma'am," said Willie, nestling close to the side of his new friend, and leaning his head upon her shoulder.

Just then the gentleman, who had been talking with the other children, approached, and said pleasantly, —

"Why, you seem to have made friends with the little boy very easily."

"Yes, indeed, for he says I look like his mother."

"How would you like to have her for a mother, Willie?" asked the gentleman, stroking the little boy's curly head. "Will you go and live with us in our home in the western country, and be our own little boy?"

The lady looked gratefully at her husband as he made this proposal, and waited eagerly for Willie's reply.

The tears came into his eyes, and he looked first at one and then at the other of his new friends, as if he was trying to decide.

At length he said, —

"If Mrs. Allen is willing, I will go. She was always kind to mother and to me, and I must mind what she says. I don't love to live here, now my mother has gone to heaven, and I should like to be your little boy."

"Well, then, we will talk to Mrs. Allen, and see what she says about it," replied the gentleman; and leaving Willie, he went with his wife into the cottage.

Good Mrs. Allen heard their proposition to take the child with great surprise, and seemed to know not what answer to make.

"We are wealthy," said the gentleman, "and have a very pleasant home in the western country. We have no children, and my wife has often proposed to me to adopt some little orphan, but I have never felt willing to do so until I saw your little Willie. If you are willing to give him up we will do well by him, and you will, I think, fulfil your promise to his mother as faithfully as if you kept him yourself."

"I think so myself, sir," answered Mrs. Allen, wiping her eyes, for she felt grieved at the thought of parting with the child. "It is little indeed that I can do for him, for in these times it is hard to keep soul and body together. And yet I hardly like to give him up to——"

"Strangers," added the lady, gently, as Mrs.

Allen hesitated. "It is very natural and very proper that you should feel so, my friend, but I do assure you, most solemnly, that I will be a kind and faithful mother to the child."

"I do not doubt it, ma'am. I see it in your face; and the gentleman will be a father to him also, and he will need one bad enough, poor thing. Squire Hall did talk about getting a pension for him by and by, but I have not much faith in it, for there will be many a pension wanting if this war keeps on. I think I will let him go, if he likes the thought himself. I cannot force him to leave me."

"Certainly not," replied the gentleman. "We will call him, and see what he has to say about it."

So Willie was called, and Mrs. Allen asked him if he would like to go far away and live with the lady and gentleman, and he again replied that he should, if she was willing; adding earnestly, —

"If I may take my mother's little Bible and my slate and pencil with me."

"You can take anything you please, dear," was the kind reply.

The gentleman then explained to Mrs. Allen that they should be obliged to take the child with them immediately, as they were to take the night train for the West, at the neighboring town.

"He will need no clothing excepting the suit which you wish him to wear," he continued, "as we shall provide suitably for him."

"But there are some things in the house which belong to him," said Mrs. Allen. "All that would sell was sold, but some things were left, and those I brought here."

"Keep all excepting such little remembrances of his parents as you think the child would most value," replied the gentleman. "He will need nothing more."

Little Willie's parcel was soon made up, — he was neatly dressed in his best suit, and after an affectionate good-by to Mrs. Allen and the children, was lifted into the carriage where the lady was already seated.

"One thing more," said the gentleman, as he was about to step in himself; "I will give you my card, Mrs. Allen, with my name and address; and then if at any time any relatives of the child should appear, they will know where to find me."

"There is little danger of that, sir," was the reply; but the gentleman took a card from his pocket-book and handed it to the good woman, and at the same time pressed into her hand a bank-note.

Then, without waiting for her thanks, he stepped into the carriage, and in another moment they were driven rapidly away.

Another year passed away. Mrs. Allen continued to occupy the same cottage, and there were new neighbors in what had once been the home of Mr. Benton and his family.

It was near the close of a summer's afternoon, and Mrs. Allen was sitting on the step of the cottage door, enjoying the cool breeze, and watching the sports of the children who were playing near her, when she observed a stranger slowly winding his way up the narrow path which led to the cottage. He was dressed in soldier's clothes; and as he drew nearer, she observed that he looked very pale and feeble, as if he had suffered much, either from wounds or ill-health. She thought, also, that there was something familiar in his face and form; but it was not until he stood directly before her, extending his hand, and saying, "Do you not know me, Mrs. Allen?" that she recognized one whom she had so long believed to be dead — the father of little Willie.

The good woman was so overcome by surprise and emotion that she could not speak a word, but held out her hand, which Mr. Benton grasped warmly.

"I see you know me now," he said. "It is not strange that you did not recognize me at first, for I must have sadly changed. Where is my dear boy, Mrs. Allen? I have been told of the death of my wife, and that you had kindly protected my poor Willie, but I do not see him among your children. Surely, surely, he has not gone from me also!" and the poor man leaned against the door for support, and groaned aloud.

"No, no, Mr. Benton, not so; sit down, and I will tell you all about it;" and rousing herself at the sight of his grief, Mrs. Allen brought a chair from the cottage, and kindly bade him be seated.

"And now, Mr. Benton, you must not blame me," she said earnestly, "for indeed I did what I thought would be best for little Willie. You know we all believed you to be dead."

"Yes, I was left for dead on the field of battle, but life was not really gone, and I was taken prisoner. I have suffered everything, Mrs. Allen, but I could have forgotten it all if my wife and child had only been here to welcome my return;" and again the poor worn-out soldier buried his face in his hands, and seemed overcome with grief.

"Take comfort," said Mrs. Allen, wiping her own eyes; "your wife was like an angel while she lived in this world, and now she has gone to be with them."

"But my boy, Mrs. Allen, if he still lives, where is he? I do so long to hold him in my arms once more."

Thus urged, Mrs. Allen told the whole story, and the father listened with eager interest.

As she concluded, the good woman again said, "You must not blame me, Mr. Benton. The child was lonely with us. You know very well that we are more like poor folks than you and your wife ever were, and Willie did not take to us kindly. And then it was very hard struggling along, and I felt afraid that we might all come to want. And the stranger gentleman seemed so good and kind, and the sweet lady spoke so gently. Willie loved her, Mr. Benton, and said she was like his mother. So I let the child go; and as we parted, the gentleman slipped a fifty dollar bill into my hand. How much it helped us, and how often I have prayed for a blessing upon him for his kindness! But I did not expect it — indeed I did not, Mr. Benton. I would never have thought of *selling* little Willie."

Mr. Benton had seemed to be lost in deep thought; but he now roused himself and said, —

"Where is the card that the stranger left with you, Mrs. Allen, with his name and address upon it? I think you said that he gave it to you."

"And so he did, for he said some one might be asking for the child; but it seemed to me that there was no chance of this, and I was so flustered when I found that he had given me a fifty dollar bill, that, to tell you the truth, I never thought of the card for two or three days, and then I could find nothing of it. I must have dropped it somewhere."

"And can you not remember the name, or where they lived?" asked Mr. Benton.

"The name I never asked, and I did not read the card. He lived out West somewhere, in Ohio, I think; yes, I am quite sure it was Ohio."

And with this unsatisfactory information Mr.

Benton was obliged to be content. He did not blame Mrs. Allen, for he felt that she had done what she believed to be her duty.

After considering the matter, and consulting with others, he decided to go at once to Ohio, and try to obtain employment somewhere in the central part of the State. He then intended to put such an advertisement in all the principal papers as would be likely to obtain for him some information respecting the child, if the gentleman who had taken him was really a resident of Ohio.

This plan he carried into effect, and in a short time he had found employment in one of the most flourishing cities in the State.

Late one afternoon, when the usual business of the day was at an end, he took a walk on the outskirts of the city, for he had as yet had but little leisure to look around, and there was much that was new and interesting to be seen.

As he walked along, he thought a good deal of his advertisement which he was intending to put in the papers the next day. Finally he took a pencil and slip of paper from his pocket, and seating himself at the foot of a majestic old oak, began to write. He was now upon the grounds belonging to a very pleasant country seat; but as the house stood far back from the road, and the place where he was sitting was very retired, he thought he should be quite unobserved.

He had been writing but a few moments when a slight noise attracted his attention, and looking up he saw seated at the foot of another tree, at a short distance from him, a pleasant looking little boy, who, like himself, was busy with a pencil and piece of paper.

"What a dear little fellow," thought Mr. Benton, with a sigh. "He must be just about the age of my Willie. I wonder what he is doing."

The boy seemed equally curious to know what the stranger was doing, for he frequently raised his eyes, and looked at him very earnestly.

At length Mr. Benton spoke to him.

"What is your name, my little fellow?"

"Willie Atwood, sir," was the reply. "I am drawing a picture. Are you drawing one?"

"No, my little man, I was writing," replied Mr. Benton, smiling at the artless simplicity of the child. "But I should like to see your picture. I had a little boy once and he used to draw pictures for me. His name was Willie, too," and Mr. Benton again sighed.

"Did your Willie die?" asked the child gently.

"No, dear, he did not die. But tell me where you live. Is it in that large house yonder?"

"Yes, sir, I live there with my father and mother. I am all the little boy they have got."

"They must love you very much, Willie. But will you not show me the picture?"

"Yes, sir, I have just finished it. Now I will show it to you;" and as the child spoke, he rose and brought his paper to the stranger.

Mr. Benton gazed at the picture with great surprise. It seemed to him a perfect representation of the cottage where he had once lived so happily with his wife and child. Even the wren-house which he had taken so much pleasure in building for his little Willie, was distinctly visible on its tall pole not far from the cottage door. An elm-tree shaded the cottage, and a little boy was sitting on the step of the door. It was a wonderful drawing for so young a child, but Mr. Benton thought not of the beauty of the drawing. It was the scene represented, that so excited his wonder.

Before he had sufficiently recovered from his surprise to ask any questions, the little boy said, —

"That is a picture of my old home. That is the wren-house which my father made for me," he continued, pointing with his finger, "and this is me sitting on the door-step watching for my father to come from his work. He had not gone to the war then."

Mr. Benton grew more and more bewildered. "Did you not say that your father lives in that large house?" he said at last, speaking with difficulty.

"Yes, my *new* father, Mr. Atwood," replied the child, "but I am telling you about my *old* father. He was killed in the war."

"And what was *his* name, Willie?" said Mr. Benton, hardly able to restrain himself from clasping the child to his heart, for he already felt sure that he had found his lost Willie.

"My name was Willie Benton, then," was the reply. "My father was Mr. Benton; I think he looked like you, only he was not so thin and pale."

Willie had no time to say more, for he found himself in the arms of the stranger, and felt somewhat alarmed at his kisses and embraces.

"Do you not know me, my darling? I am your father come back from the war."

"And is my mother here too?" exclaimed the child. "They told me you were both in heaven. Oh, I am so glad!" and little Willie clasped his arms around his father's neck, and sobbed for joy.

"Your mother is in heaven, my own dear boy, but I was taken prisoner, and not killed, as was supposed. When I got home and found that your dear mother had died, and that you had gone far away, I came to this State to look for you. But are you happy where you are, Willie? Are Mr. and Mrs. Atwood kind to you?"

"Oh, very, very kind," said Willie. "They love me dearly, and I love them. Come now, and I will show you to them," he continued, taking his father's hand and trying to draw him along.

"I fear they will not be so glad to see me as you are, Willie," replied Mr. Benton, rising, and walking along with the little boy.

"Oh, they will, I am very sure. Mother always talks to me of you and of my own dear mother, and she reads to me from the same little Bible, and hears me say my prayers."

Mr. and Mrs. Atwood did indeed give Mr. Benton a hearty welcome, although they felt grieved at the thought that their adopted child, to whom they both felt most tenderly attached, might be taken from them. But Mr. Benton was too sensible a man not to see the advantages of such a home for his child. He knew how much Willie must miss the love and care of his mother, and he saw that Mrs. Atwood had in a great measure supplied that mother's place. He was therefore easily persuaded by Mr. Atwood to allow Willie to remain with them, while he was so situated as to see him daily. Mr. Atwood was wealthy and influential, and he easily obtained an excellent situation for Mr. Benton, well suited to his tastes and capacity.

Willie loved both his *old* father and his *new* father very dearly; and while he often thought and spoke of his dear mother in heaven, he was very happy under the care of the new mother whom the Lord had so mercifully provided for him.

SIXTY MINUTES MAKE ONE HOUR.

"Sixty seconds make a minute,
  Time enough to tie my shoe;
Sixty minutes make an hour,
  Shall it pass with naught to do?"

THUS sung little Mary Goodwin, as she entered the parlor where her father and mother were sitting one pleasant summer morning; but she stopped when she saw that her father was reading the newspaper, for she had been taught to carefully avoid interrupting others. She stood by her father's side, waiting patiently till he was ready to attend to her.

Presently, he laid the paper upon the table, and said, "Well, my daughter, are you going to school?"

"Yes, father," replied Mary. "Will you please to give me my motto for this week?"

Mr. Goodwin was in the habit of giving his little girl a motto every Monday morning, which she could in some way apply to her conduct during the week. He had been reading so busily, that he had forgotten to select one that morning, and when Mary reminded him of it, he hesitated for a few moments, as if at a loss what to say.

"The verse that Mary was singing would make a good motto," remarked Mrs. Goodwin, as she called Mary to her side, and smoothed back her hair, and tied her cape-bonnet more neatly, for she was a careless little girl, and seldom remembered to pin her shawl even, or tie her bonnet in a nice bow-knot. One corner of the shawl frequently hung a quarter of a yard below the other, and the bonnet was sometimes not tied at all, or, at best, there was but one bow to be seen, while the other string hung carelessly at the side.

"Why mother," exclaimed Mary, "what a funny motto! I should not learn anything new from that. Everybody knows that sixty seconds make a minute, and that sixty minutes make an hour."

"A great many people know it, but very few recollect it in a way to make the knowledge of any use to them," replied her father. "I think it will be an excellent motto for you, and for your brother Frank also. Indeed, it would do us all good to remember that even one minute of time is long enough to enable us to do something useful to ourselves or others, if it is only to tie a shoe."

"That is not very useful, father," said Mary, laughing. "It is a very small use."

"And a minute is but a very small portion of time," replied Mr. Goodwin; "but if we perform a small use, as you call it, every minute, we shall find that we have been of very great use at the end of a day."

Mary still looked a little dissatisfied with her motto, and said she should not know how to apply it.

"I will tell you one way," said her father, "and when you have put that into practice, we will think of other ways. Every time that you are tempted to be idle for a few seconds or minutes in school to-day, remember your motto, and try to spend every instant in learning or doing something useful. I suppose you would think it very wrong if you should see one of your school-mates pass an hour in idleness or play, when she ought to attend to her lessons; but, if you are watchful of yourself, you will find that you often neglect your studies for a few minutes, without thinking that you are doing wrong; but recollect that if you do this several times in the course of a day, the number of minutes will soon amount to sixty, and then one misspent hour will have gone, never to return."

Mary had read a little book called the *Well-Spent Hour*, and when her father spoke of a *misspent* hour, it brought this story to her mind, and she said, "Father, I will try to have all my minutes well-spent minutes, and all my hours well-spent hours."

"That is a good resolution," replied her father, kissing her affectionately; "and now go to school, and this evening you may tell me if you have found your motto of use to you during the day."

As Mary left the house she met her brother Frank, who had been of an errand for his father. He had a large package of books in his hands.

"Please to run up the steps again, Mary, and open the door for me," said he. "It will delay you but a minute."

"And it will do some good," said Mary; and she told her brother about her motto, and that she meant to try to improve every minute through the day. Frank was two years older than Mary, a fine, intelligent boy of eleven, and he said he believed he knew several ways in which it would be useful to them to recollect this motto, but, as it was nearly time for school to begin, it would not do to talk about it then. So they bade each other good morning, and Mary walked quickly away, for she did not wish to grieve her teacher by being late.

Miss Ainsworth was very desirous to have all her pupils punctual, and was always careful to set them a good example herself, by being at the school-house in season, and having everything prepared for the duties of the day before nine o'clock, at which hour school commenced.

As Mary was tripping merrily along, she saw one of her school-mates at a short distance before her. She was a pleasant little girl, named Ellen Brown, and Mary was glad to overtake her.

Ellen was so busily engaged in picking blackberries, that she did not see Mary until she stood close by her side.

"O, Mary!" she exclaimed, "you almost frightened me. I did not hear your step. See what nice ripe berries I have found. Stop a few minutes and help me fill the basket, and then I will give you half of all I have gathered."

"Thank you," said Mary, looking with much pleasure at a small basket which Ellen held in her hand, about half full of large ripe berries; and she laid her book and slate under a tree, and began to help Ellen.

"I have done all my sums," said Ellen, who was in the same class in arithmetic as Mary; "and our table is very easy this morning. It is about time, and we can almost say it without studying. Sixty seconds make a minute, sixty minutes make an hour, twenty-four hours make a ——"

But here Ellen was interrupted by Mary, who, hastily tossing the berries she had gathered into the basket, took her book and slate, and said, —

"Come, Ellen, I must go this moment. We shall be late at school."

"Why, Mary, we have not filled the basket yet. You said you would help me." And Ellen looked a little displeased at Mary's abrupt manner.

"I remembered my motto for this week," replied Mary. "Sixty seconds make a minute. Time enough to tie my shoe. You know the verse, Ellen. I cannot stop now, because father told me to try not to waste a moment of time to-day. I will ask mother to let me pick berries after school."

"They will all be gone then," said Ellen; but she took her basket and followed Mary, and they walked along together, talking about the motto.

"You know, Ellen," said Mary, "that often when we think we will stop but a few minutes, the time passes so quickly and pleasantly that we stay much longer than we intended. Now as it takes but sixty minutes to make an hour, if we waste a few minutes this morning, and a few more several times in the course of the day, an hour will soon be gone, never to return, as father told me this morning."

Ellen had recovered her good-humor, and she told Mary that she would still give her half of the berries, and that if their mothers were willing, they could go to Blackberry Hill after school in the afternoon, and there they could gather a quart in a short time.

The girls had now reached the school-house. It was a very neat little building, with a small garden in front, which the scholars took great delight in cultivating, and it was now full of beautiful flowers. Behind the school-house there was a small enclosure for a play-ground, which was beautifully shaded by two large elm-trees.

Mary and Ellen were glad that they had not stopped any longer to gather berries, for their teacher stood at the door with a small bell in her hand, and, as soon as she had bade them good morning, she rung it loudly, so that all the scholars who were on the play-ground, or in any of the pleasant lanes near the house, could hear it. In a few minutes a great many little girls were seen hastening along from different directions, and very soon they were all quietly seated at their desks with their Bibles open before them, ready for morning worship. Just then, the old-fashioned clock, which stood in the corner of the room, struck nine, for Miss Ainsworth always rung the bell when the hand pointed to ten minutes of nine, and this gave the girls time to take off their bonnets and shawls, and take their seats in an orderly manner before the proper hour for school to commence.

Mary frequently thought of her motto during the day, and found it very useful in reminding her not to be idle, and also in some other ways. Once it prevented her from saying what was not strictly true. The class in geography had a lesson to learn which was quite difficult, and their teacher requested them to study it diligently for an hour. When the class was called to recite, Miss Ainsworth said, "How many of you have studied this lesson an hour?" Nearly all the girls raised their hands to show that they had done so, and Mary was about raising hers, when she recollected her motto, "Sixty minutes make an hour," and she said, "I do not think that I have studied quite sixty minutes, for I looked out of the window once or twice."

Her teacher told her that she was glad she was so careful to speak the exact truth, and several of the girls who had raised their hands, when they heard what Mary said, and remembered how many minutes it took to make an hour, acknowledged that they had not studied quite an hour. Thus Mary not only did what was right herself, but helped others to do so also.

Another time she had forgotten her motto, and was busily engaged in cutting figures out of a bit of colored paper which she had found on her desk, when a very little girl, who sat on a low seat near to her, whispered, "Mary, please to tie my shoe." These words reminded Mary of her resolution to perform some use, however small, every minute in the day, and she blushed to think she should have so soon forgotten it. She put away her paper, and for the rest of the day was very studious and industrious.

After school in the afternoon she had a pleasant walk with Ellen to Blackberry Hill, and took a large basket of berries home to her mother.

She was glad when it was evening, so that she might talk with her father about her motto, and as soon as the lamps were lighted, she ran for her brother Frank, who was sitting in the kitchen making a boat, and said, "Come, Frank, let us go into the parlor now, and talk with father."

"In one minute, Mary," replied Frank, "as soon as I have smoothed this bowsprit. Wait for me just one minute."

Mary waited five minutes, and still Frank was not ready, and she began to be impatient.

"You forget that sixty seconds make a minute," she said. "It is not right to say that you will be ready in one minute, when you mean five or ten."

"That is what my teacher would call a very just observation," replied Frank, smiling; and he put away his boat and tools, and went with Mary into the parlor.

Then Mary told her father in what ways she had found her motto useful through the day. "Was it not strange, father," she asked, "that whenever I was in danger of forgetting my motto, something would always happen to remind me of it? This morning, when I stopped on my way to school to pick berries, Ellen began to repeat the table of time which was in our arithmetic lesson for to-day, and that reminded me of my motto. Another time, when I was playing in school, little Clara Winslow asked me to tie her shoe, which brought the verse to my mind at once."

"I do not think this was strange, Mary," replied her father, "although it is certainly very affecting and delightful to think how constantly the Lord watches over us, and endeavors to lead us to do right. You know that the good spirits around you are always imparting to you good thoughts and feelings, and trying to make you good and happy. To-day you were really in the desire to be led by them, and to employ your time usefully; and when you sometimes forgot your resolution for a few moments, the angels who were guarding you from evil, induced your companions to say something which brought your motto to your mind, and thus reminded you of your duty."

Mary did not reply to what her father said, but her heart was filled with gratitude to the Lord for His goodness in keeping His angels around her to guard her from evil, and she prayed that she might be led wholly by them.

Frank broke the silence by saying that he had observed one way in which it would be useful for every one to remember the motto. He had been to a large town that day on some business for his father, and he related several instances of want of punctuality and exactness in keeping promises. One gentleman from whom he was to receive some money, told him to call in an hour from the time he first went there, and he would have it ready for him.

Frank called at the proper time, but the gentleman had gone out, and he was obliged to wait nearly another hour, before he could receive the money.

"I thought he had forgotten how many minutes

it takes to make an hour," said Frank; "and very soon I met with another gentleman, who really did not appear to know how many seconds it takes to make a minute, for when I delivered your note to him, father, he said, 'Sit down a minute, my boy, and I will attend to you,' and he kept me waiting more than half an hour."

Mary laughed a little as Frank said this, for she remembered how he had kept her waiting while he worked on his boat, and Frank smiled also, for he thought of the same thing.

"It is very common to say that we will be ready in a minute, when we mean a somewhat longer time," said Mr. Goodwin, "but it is much better to try to speak the exact truth in this, as in all things. The principal way, however, in which I wish your motto to be useful to you, is in reminding you of the great importance of improving every minute of your time. It is wrong to waste even the smallest portion of time, for even one minute is often sufficient to enable us to perform some act of usefulness. Only think how much good we could do in a year if we rightly improved every minute!"

"Do you suppose any person ever improved every minute of a year, father?" asked Frank.

"I think not, Frank, but some persons come much nearer doing so than others. We should regard our time as belonging to the Lord, and to be spent in such a way as to enable us to become mediums of His good and truth; that is, we should constantly try to learn and do what will make us the most useful in this world, and hereafter in the spiritual world. The love of use constitutes the happiness of the angels of heaven."

"Then the more we try to be useful, the more we become like the angels, do we not, father?" asked Mary.

"Certainly," replied her father. "The angels are continually endeavoring to lead us to perform uses, and the more we suffer ourselves to be led by them, the more like them we become."

"And when we die we shall be happy with them, forever. That is what my catechism says," said Mary. "I should like to be an angel, father, and I will try to improve every moment in learning and doing something useful."

"And so will I try," said Frank; "but we shall

forget very often, Mary. It is not a very easy lesson to learn, is it, father?"

"Indeed it is not, my son," replied Mr. Goodwin, "it is very difficult, and we must humbly look to the Lord for help. Without His aid we cannot even try to do good. And now good-night, my children, and may the Lord enable you to keep your good resolutions."

Mary rose at an early hour the next morning, with her thoughts filled with the resolution to usefully employ every moment. But she met with difficulties which somewhat discouraged her. We have already spoken of her careless habits, and these she found very troublesome now that she was endeavoring not to waste the smallest portion of time. Even while dressing in the morning, she was delayed nearly half an hour, because her clothes were not in proper order. One article wanted a button and another a string, and she was obliged to stop to sew them on. Then one shoestring was missing, and after searching for it some time, Mary recollected having seen her shoe untied while walking with Ellen the day before; and as she had neglected to tie it then, it was probably lost before she reached home. She applied to her mother for another, which she gave her, at the same time reminding her that even one minute was sufficient to tie a shoe, and thus the loss could generally be avoided.

All these little troubles took so much time, that the breakfast bell rung before Mary was quite ready, and she felt hurried and disturbed, and did not derive the benefit from family worship which she would have done, had her mind been in a calm and pleasant state. Many other troubles resulting from her careless habits occurred during the day, and she returned from school feeling very sad, and told her mother that she feared she should never be like the angels, for she had done very little that was useful that day.

"I am sorry to hear it, Mary," replied her mother, "but you must not be discouraged by one failure. We all fail many times in our efforts to become good. Come with me now and help me prepare our tea, and this evening we will talk of your troubles, and try to ascertain the cause of them."

Mary was glad to be of any use, and she moved briskly around, assisting her mother in every possible way until tea was upon the table.

In the evening her father and brother attended a scientific lecture in the neighborhood, and Mary took her sewing, and seated herself by her mother's side.

"I have wasted a great deal of time to-day, mother," she said. "This morning I rose very early that I might help you before I went to school, but everything went wrong. My clothes were not in order, and some things were out of place, and it took me a long time to find them. At school there was the same trouble. My slate pencil was not in the little box which you gave me to keep it in, and I looked for it a long time in vain. At last I found it in a book in which I was reading yesterday. I remember leaving it there for a mark. Then I felt in a hurry about my sums, and therefore did many of them wrong. When Miss Ainsworth handed me my slate, she said, 'The mistakes in your sums are entirely from carelessness, Mary. You evidently know how to do them.'

"This was true; for when I looked them over, I found that in some places in subtraction, I had placed the greater number under the smaller, which I am sure I knew to be wrong.

"When the hour for sewing arrived, I intended

to be very industrious, but I was obliged to leave my seat for a moment, and carelessly left my needle hanging loosely from my work. When I returned, my work had fallen from the desk, and the needle was gone. It took me full fifteen minutes to find it.

"I could tell you a great many more troubles, mother, but they are all much alike."

"And may all be attributed to one cause, may they not, Mary?" asked her mother.

"I suppose they may, mother. My carelessness, which you have so often talked to me about, is the true cause of all my difficulties to-day. I find that I can never learn to employ every moment usefully until I learn to be orderly and careful in my habits. But, mother, is it not strange that the angels have not helped me to do right to-day? I am sure I have thought of my motto, and should have been glad to have improved my time."

"There are many ways in which the angels help us, dear Mary, even when we are the least sensible of their presence. Before you can become useful to yourself or others, it is necessary that you should be brought into a state in which you can see the evil of your careless and disorderly habits. Your father and I have often talked to you about this fault, and endeavored to help you to put it away; but it has been difficult to make you aware of it yourself, and little improvement has been made. The good spirits around you have evidently been endeavoring to-day to bring you to an acknowledgment of this evil, and for this purpose it was necessary that you should meet with some troubles."

"But I feel so sorry, mother, that I have lost a day. I meant to be so very useful."

"The day is far from being lost, if you are really convinced of the sin of carelessness. It may truly be called a sin, because it prevents us from doing many good actions, and is the cause of much trouble and inconvenience to those around us. If you are now fully aware that this is one of your faults, and are sincerely resolved to correct it, you may regard this as one of the most useful days of your life."

Mary's countenance brightened at this view of the case, and she said earnestly, "I do mean to try to be orderly and careful, dear mother. I will begin to-morrow, and you shall see how much I will improve in a week."

"Begin to-night, Mary," replied her mother,

smiling; "be sure that all your clothes are in order for the morning, so that the misfortunes of to-day may be avoided. A short time ago, I put everything belonging to you in neat order; but now all is confusion again. But as you are resolved to do better, I will help you as much as possible. I will show you a place for everything, and you must remember to keep everything in its proper place."

"That is a difficult rule to obey, mother. I am so often tempted to lay my things down for a moment, and then I forget to put them away. But I will try. I will remember the motto that I had a few weeks ago: 'Patience and perseverance accomplish all things.'"

"Yes, you may remember that, Mary, but, above all, remember to look to the Lord for help to enable you to put away this and all your evils. If you trust to your own strength, you can do nothing."

"I will pray to Him to help me," said Mary, "and I will thank Him for His goodness in keeping His angels around me to show me my faults, and to help me put them away."

Her mother kissed her, and advised her to go to her own room then, that she might have time to arrange her clothes properly, and to read in the Word before her usual hour for going to rest.

The next three days were happy ones. Mary kept her resolution to endeavor to be orderly, and she found that thus much time was saved, and she could do many useful things which she formerly thought she had no time to do. It is true that she sometimes indulged in her former careless habits, but a word from her mother was sufficient to remind her of her resolution, and encourage her to persevere.

Her parents and her brother Frank were much pleased with the change.

"I have not found any of your things in my way for two or three days, Mary," said Frank. "You are really becoming very orderly. Your books are all neatly arranged on your shelves, your workbasket is in its place, and I have observed that your bonnet and shawl are neatly put on when you go out. What has changed you so suddenly?"

"Why, Frank," replied Mary, "I found that I could never learn to employ every minute usefully, until I became more orderly, for I wasted a great deal of time in looking for things which were out of place. Even pinning my shawl and tying my bonnet carelessly wasted time, for mother always called me to her, and fixed them properly. You have no idea how many things I find time to do now. See this silk handkerchief which I have nearly hemmed for father, and this pretty purse which I am knitting for somebody!"

"For me, perhaps," said Frank, examining his sister's work with pleasure.

"I shall not tell you," replied Mary. "You will know in proper time; but I must bid you good-morning, Frank, for it is nearly school time. To-day is Friday, the last day of school for this week, and to-morrow mother has promised that I shall visit cousin Emily if I am a good girl."

Saturday proved a day of trial to Mary. The morning was cloudy, and soon after breakfast it began to rain. Mary had anticipated much pleasure from her visit to her cousin, and she was quite unprepared for the disappointment. She stood at the window watching the clouds for a few minutes, and then said, "It does not rain very hard, mother. If I take an umbrella I shall not get wet. May I go?"

"No, Mary," replied her mother. "You have quite a bad cold, and it is a long walk to your uncle's. I think it would be wrong to allow you to go in the rain. I am sorry for your disappointment; but as it cannot be avoided, I advise you to think no more of your visit, but try to spend your holiday usefully and happily at home."

But Mary felt sad and displeased, and was not disposed to comply with her mother's advice. She still sat by the window watching the drops of rain which fell against the glass, and indulged her illhumor by making fretful and unpleasant remarks.

"It always rains when I wish to go anywhere," she said. "I wish it would rain some other day than Saturday. Now I must wait another week for my visit, and then, I dare say, it will rain again."

Mrs. Goodwin took little notice of Mary, hoping that she would suffer the angels to draw near to her, and help her to put away the evil state. But after some time had passed, and she still continued in the same fretful mood, she said, —

"You have forgotten your good resolutions, Mary. You have passed the last half hour worse than uselessly. Our Heavenly Father knows what is best for us. He maketh the sun to shine and the rain to fall. When we fret about the weather, we murmur against the Lord."

Mary was not an obstinate child. She felt the truth of her mother's words, and frankly acknowledged her fault.

"I will try not to think of my visit any more," she said. "What can I do to help me to forget it, mother?"

"When we feel sad from any cause, the best remedy is to employ ourselves in trying to make others happy," replied Mrs. Goodwin. "If we do this from a sincere love of doing good, we shall always find that the happiness we are endeavoring to impart to others, is received by ourselves also."

"Well, mother," said Mary, cheerfully, "I will help you all I can, and I will cover Frank's ball, and make a frock for sister Ella's new doll."

Little Ella was standing by a chair upon which she had placed her little cups and saucers, and when she heard Mary speak of dressing her doll, she looked up very much pleased. Her bright smile made Mary feel that it is indeed true that giving pleasure to others makes our own hearts happy; and she thought no more of the rain and her disappointment, but employed herself usefully and happily all the morning.

Her mother's cares were lightened. Frank's old ball was so neatly covered, that it looked like a new one, and a pretty little frock was made for Ella's doll. At one o'clock, when the bell called her to dinner, Mary was surprised to observe that the rain had ceased, and the sun was dimly shining through the clouds.

Soon after they were seated at the table, her father told her that he was going to a town at some distance, and would take her to her uncle's in the chaise, and call for her at an early hour in the evening.

The afternoon passed very pleasantly; the more so because evil feelings had been conquered in the morning, and acts of usefulness and kindness had been performed.

Mary told her cousin about her motto, and of the use it had been to her through the week, and they both resolved to remember that even one minute is time enough to do some good, and that sixty well-spent minutes make a well-spent hour.

THE LOST KNIFE;
OR,
BEARING FALSE WITNESS.

"WHAT are you trying to make, Willie?" said Alfred Goodwin, as he came from school one afternoon, and found his little brother seated upon the door-step whittling a stick with an old case-knife which he had persuaded his mother to lend him for a little while.

"I am trying to make a windmill," replied Willie; and with a great effort he succeeded in cutting quite a shaving with the dull old knife. As he did this, he looked up at Alfred with a smile, which seemed to say, "Did you see me do that? Wasn't that a big shaving?"

"I will make you a windmill, if you like, Willie," said Alfred, good-naturedly; "I am used to making windmills, and so I can make good ones."

Willie gratefully accepted the offer, and handed Alfred his knife and sticks; but Alfred said he could find wood that would suit him better, in the barn; and as for the knife, Willie had better carry it back to his mother, as he would rather use his own jack-knife.

Some soft pieces of smooth pine-wood were soon found, for Alfred always kept a good stock on hand, and then he felt in his pocket for his knife. It was certainly not in his usual pocket, but perhaps he had accidentally slipped it into another. Both pants and jacket were carefully searched, but all in vain; no knife was to be found.

"Now where can that knife be!" exclaimed Alfred, looking much perplexed. "Let me think. I have not had it to-day, but yesterday I made whistles at recess. Oh, now I remember! I lent it to Joe Williams, and I suppose he forgot to give it back to me. I will ask him for it this afternoon. Run and ask father, Willie, to please to lend Alfred his sharp knife to make you a windmill."

The little boy ran cheerfully away, and in a few

moments returned with the knife. A pretty windmill was soon made, and all the litter cleared up, and the knife given back to their father, before the dinner-bell rang.

Joseph Williams was Alfred's most intimate friend, and, as they walked home from school together as usual that afternoon, Alfred happened to think of his knife, and said suddenly,—

"O! where is my knife, Joe? You forgot to give it to me."

"I do not think I have had it to-day, have I, Alf?"

"No, not to-day, but yesterday, to make a whistle; don't you recollect?"

"Yes, I recollect having it to make a whistle; but I am sure I gave it back to you."

"No you didn't. I have not had it since, and I have searched all my pockets; so please search yours."

This was said pleasantly, and Joseph immediately complied; he turned his pockets inside out, but no knife appeared.

"I am sure I gave it back to you," he repeated, as the last pocket was searched.

"And I am sure you did not," returned Alfred,

positively. "I always keep my knife in the right-hand pocket of my pants, and it is not there, nor in any of my other pockets. You must have lost it somewhere."

Joseph felt somewhat indignant at this hasty speech; and as they came just then to the road which led to his own home, he turned quickly away, and walked in that direction, instead of going a little farther with Alfred, as was his usual custom.

This added to Alfred's ill-humor; and he muttered to himself, as he walked along, "So mean to sneak off in that way! If he has lost the knife, why can't he say so, honestly."

The next few days made matters worse between the two friends. Alfred was a great favorite with his school-fellows, on account of his cheerful, obliging disposition, and the pleasant frankness of his manners. Joseph was more reserved, and by no means so universally liked. As soon, therefore, as it was whispered among the little circle that "Joe had got Alfred's knife," great indignation was felt.

"I never did like the fellow," said one, "he

always seemed so proud and stuck-up. I wonder what made Alf think so much of him?"

"So mean in him to borrow a knife, and then say he gave it back, when, no doubt, he lost it," said another.

"No, he has not *lost it*," said a third, with a mysterious look and manner. "I know something about that."

"What do you know? Tell us, Mark, that's a good fellow," cried the others, crowding around him.

"I know that he has it in his pocket," replied Mark, with an air of importance. "Yesterday afternoon I passed by his house, and as he was standing in the wood-shed, cutting sticks, I stopped to see what he was making. He had a brown-handled knife in his hand, and as I looked at it I could not help exclaiming, 'Why, there is Alf's knife!' for it really looked precisely like it. Joe colored as red as a beet, and put the knife in his pocket, saying, in a very short way, 'No, it is'nt Alf's knife! It is mine.' But I know it *is* Alf's."

"Of course it is," responded the eager listeners. "If Alf will give us leave, we will make him give it up."

But Alfred would not consent to any violence.

"If Joe is so mean as to take the knife in that way, he may keep it," he said, contemptuously; "I will have nothing more to do with him. I don't care for the knife," he added, "for my uncle made me a present of a very good one yesterday, as it was my birth-day. Joe might have had the other, and welcome; but he couldn't wait for me to give it to him."

In spite of Alfred's expressed wish that no violence should be used, many sly tricks were played upon Joseph, and many an insulting remark made in his presence, all of which he bore in silence, treating his persecutors as if he considered them quite unworthy of notice.

In reality, however, he suffered much from the loss of Alfred's friendship, for his parents were poor, while Alfred's were more wealthy; and, being pleased with the appearance of the boy whom their son had chosen for a friend, they had encouraged the intimacy, and shown Joseph many acts of kindness.

Alfred also felt the change, for Joseph was somewhat older than himself, and a very excellent scholar, and he had depended a good deal upon him for assistance in his studies.

Thus several weeks passed away very uncomfortably to both parties, and yet neither were in the slightest degree inclined to yield. Alfred remained firm in his opinion that "Joe took the knife," and Joseph was equally firm in his resolution to make no attempt at an explanation, but to treat the whole affair with contempt.

Alfred's mother was from home during the greater part of this time, or she would have noticed the change in the intimacy between the boys, and would have endeavored to have set the matter right.

Not many days after her return, she kindly inquired for Joe.

"I have not seen him since I came home," she said. "He is not sick, I hope."

"No, he is well enough," replied Alfred; "but we do not go together any more, mother."

"Do not go together any more!" repeated his mother. "You do not mean that you are no longer friends?"

"Yes, mother, that is what I mean."

"I am very sorry to hear it, Alfred," said Mrs.

Goodwin, gravely. "I fear you have been to blame. Trifles should not part friends."

"It was no trifle, mother," exclaimed Alfred, indignantly; "Joe Williams stole my knife."

"That is a serious charge, Alfred. I certainly do not wish you to associate with a dishonest boy. Have you good proof?"

"Yes, mother, of course I have. I lent it to him, and he did not give it back to me, and when I asked him for it he was huffy, and said he had not got it."

"Well, Alfred, and where is your proof that he had? You might have been mistaken."

"No, mother, I am perfectly sure that I lent it to him, and I searched all my own things for it in vain; and, besides that, mother," urged Alfred, eagerly, for he saw that his mother was still unconvinced, "Mark Stevens *saw* him have my knife."

"Ah, that alters the case," said Mrs. Goodwin. "If Joseph has really been seen with the knife in his possession, that must be taken as proof. But is Mark quite sure?"

"Yes, mother, Joe was in his own wood-shed cutting sticks with a knife which Mark says looked exactly like mine. He told him it was 'Alf's knife,' and Joe said it was not, but he colored up, and put the knife in his pocket. It must have been mine, mother, for Joe had none of his own. I always lent him mine, and should have given it to him after uncle gave me the new one, if he had not helped himself to it before that time."

Mrs. Goodwin mused in silence for a little while, and then said, —

"The circumstances are certainly suspicious, Alfred, but still I do not think the proof full and clear. It is a very serious thing to accuse any one of theft. It was your duty to have had a kind and friendly talk with Joseph, and asked him frankly where he got the knife that Mark saw him have."

"He would not have told me, mother. He treats all the boys with contempt, and will never answer any questions about the knife."

"Because his feelings have been wounded by your hasty judgment, and harsh accusations, Alfred."

"I have said nothing, I think, but what was true, mother."

"Perhaps not; but *possibly* you have, and if this should prove to be the case, you will deeply regret what you have done."

Alfred looked grave and uneasy. He was a truthful boy, in the common meaning of the term, and could not bear to think that he might possibly have told a falsehood.

His mother was called from the room just then, and no more was said on the subject.

Another week passed away, and there was still no change. Saturday afternoon came, and a large party of the school-boys had agreed to go to the woods for chestnuts. Alfred was eager to be of the number.

"It will be such fun to hear them come rattling down," he said; "can I go, mother?"

His mother gave her consent, but added, "Not in those clothes, Alfred; go and put on your gray suit, which hangs in the closet in your room."

Alfred obeyed, saying cheerfully, as he left the room, —

"That's a good suit for work or play; but it is so long since I wore it, that I am afraid it will feel rather tight."

The suit fitted nicely, in spite of his fears, however; but just as he was fairly equipped, he felt something hard in the right-hand pocket of the pants, and putting in his hand to see what it could be, pulled out the *long-lost knife*.

The whole truth flashed upon his mind. He had worn those pants one afternoon, many weeks before, to go a-fishing with Joe. He remembered it all now. He had put his knife in that pocket, and there it had been ever since. And poor Joe! How falsely he had accused him, and what could he do now? He felt so ashamed to tell his mother, and, above all, to tell all the boys. But this was only a momentary feeling. Alfred was, as we have said before, a truthful boy. He had judged hastily, and had said what was false, but now that he was convinced of his injustice, he was willing to do all in his power to make reparation.

In another moment he was at his mother's side, and had told her the whole story.

"*Thou shalt not bear false witness against thy neighbor*," she said, solemnly, but affectionately, as he ended. "It will be a lesson to you, my dear boy. Hasty judgments often lead us to commit great sins."

"I hope I shall be more careful in future. I will try, mother."

"And what will you do now, Alfred?"

"I think I will go at once to Joe, mother, and tell him the whole affair, and ask his forgiveness. He is not invited to join our party; but if he will go with me, I will show the knife to all the boys, and I am sure they will all be sorry for what they have done, and give him a hearty welcome."

"That is a good plan, my boy. Tell Joseph, from me, that I hope he will go with you. Tell him that I think it his duty."

There was great surprise among the boys when, as they had almost given up the hope of seeing Alfred, he suddenly appeared, coming towards them, arm-in-arm with his old friend Joe Williams.

As soon as he came near enough to speak, he held up the knife, and said, in a voice loud enough for all to hear, —

"This is my old knife, boys, that we have so long accused Joe of taking. I found it to-day in the pocket of these old pants, where it has been for weeks. The knife which Mark saw Joe have was given to him by a friend that very day. It *does* look something like mine, but not exactly. I have done Joe great injustice, boys, but he has kindly forgiven me, and I shall try to be a better friend in future. I am sure you are all sorry for having suspected him."

"Three cheers for Joe Williams," shouted some of the younger boys, while the older ones came forward to shake hands and express their sorrow.

The cheers were given with hearty good-will, and then all united in a vigorous attack upon the chestnut-trees.

Alfred never forgot the lesson he had learned.

When tempted to hasty judgments and harsh accusations, he would remember the lost knife, and carefully examine himself, lest he should again *bear false witness against his neighbor.*

MAKING THE BEST OF IT.

"SUCH a long spelling lesson as we have got for to-morrow," said little Julia Meredith, as she seated herself at the table one evening after supper, and placed her school-books at her side.

"Just look, mother," she continued, holding up the spelling-book so that her mother could see it, and pointing to the lesson for the next day. "All that! Isn't it too long?"

"Oh, I think you will be able to learn it, Julia," replied her mother, glancing at the lesson, which was really a long one. "Study industriously for a little while, and then I will see how many words you can spell."

"It is too long," repeated Julia, impatiently, "and I know I can never learn it. The teacher ought not to have given us such a long lesson."

After some urging from her mother, however, Julia began studying, but soon became discouraged, and again fretted at the length of the lesson. Just then her father's step was heard in the entry, and Julia sprang up to open the door for him.

Mr. Meredith had been obliged to go out for a little while after tea, but had now returned to pass the evening with his family. The younger children were asleep, but Julia was very glad to welcome her father, for he often assisted her in learning her lessons. Just now, however, she seemed to want his sympathy more than his assistance; for, as soon as he had taken his accustomed seat, she showed him the spelling lesson, and asked him if it was not a very long one.

Mr. Meredith examined it carefully, and presently replied, —

"Yes, I think it is a long lesson."

Mrs. Meredith looked up with some surprise. She had thought, herself, that the lesson was a long one, but she did not feel sure that it was wise to admit this to Julia. She made no remark, however, but went quietly on with her sewing.

"I knew you would think it was too long!" exclaimed Julia, triumphantly. "I am sure it is the longest spelling lesson that has ever been given to our class. What would you do about it, father?"

"First tell me what you have already done," replied her father.

"I told Miss Seaton that I knew I could never learn it," said Julia, "but she only smiled, and said I could not be sure till I had tried."

"And have you tried?" asked Mr. Meredith.

"Not much, for I know it would be of no use. I have a great mind not to study it at all, and just tell Miss Seaton, to-morrow, that it was a great deal too long. What would *you* do, father?"

"I think," replied her father, slowly and thoughtfully, "that I would make the best of it."

"Oh, father," exclaimed Julia, "that is what you always say when I am in any trouble."

"Because it is really the very best way to get out of trouble, my little girl. We must all have many trials, great trials and little trials, and nothing will so greatly help us to bear them, as a cheerful disposition. But now let us look at the spelling lesson, and see what can be done with it."

Julia again handed the book to her father, and after another examination, he took a lead pencil from his pocket, and marked several words.

"Can you learn twelve hard words, Julia?" he asked, as he placed the book before her.

"Oh yes, father, I can learn twelve words easily; but that would be but a small part of the lesson."

"I know that, Julia, but I have marked twelve that I wish you to learn first, and then we will talk about the rest."

Julia studied busily for a few minutes, and then told her father that she could spell all the words that he had marked.

"Then I think you will find that you can spell the whole lesson. Hand me the book, and I will put out the words to you."

Julia obeyed, and, to her great surprise, went through the whole lesson with only one slight mistake. She looked a little mortified as she met her father's smile when he closed the book.

"I really thought it was a hard lesson, father," she said.

"I have no doubt you did, Julia, but you should have examined it, and tried to make the best of it. It was a long lesson, but I saw at once that the greater part of the words were very easy."

"Now that the spelling lesson was off her mind," as Julia said, "the geography and history would soon be learned;" and when bed-time came she had the pleasure of feeling quite sure that she was well prepared for school the next day. "Father has such a nice way of helping me to learn my lessons," she said to herself, as she laid her head upon her pillow; "I am so glad that I know that spelling lesson."

Perhaps Julia thought more of having learned the spelling lesson so easily, than she did of her father's advice as to what she ought to do in all her little troubles. I think this must have been the case; for the next morning brought new trials, and it certainly did not appear that she tried to make the best of them. The first trouble was waking up half an hour later than she had intended to do. Julia was working a pair of slippers which she intended for a birthday gift to her father, and she had made a resolution to rise early in the morning, and work upon them for an hour before breakfast. She had succeeded in waking at the proper time for several mornings, and now she felt greatly disappointed when, on peeping out of her room to look at the old clock which stood at the head of the stairs, she found herself so much behind the appointed time.

"It is really too bad!" she exclaimed; "I shall not have more than half an hour to sew on the slippers, and that will not even finish the rose-bud that I begun yesterday. I will just go back to bed, and not try at all this morning." So, feeling quite vexed and out of humor, Julia crept back to bed, and lay half awake and half asleep, until the first bell rung, which was the signal for all to get up and prepare for breakfast.

Just as Julia was ready to go down stairs, her mother opened the door of her room. "Are you quite ready, Julia?" she said, pleasantly. "And how do the slippers come on?"

"I have not worked on them this morning, mother; I woke up too late, — at least it was later than I meant to wake, and I should have had but half an hour."

"That would have been better than nothing, Julia; but there is the breakfast-bell; we must go down."

Julia followed her mother, feeling rather dissatisfied with herself and all around her. Her good humor was by no means restored when she found that a gentleman who was taking breakfast with them occupied her seat at the table. To be sure there was another seat for Julia, but she preferred her accustomed place near her father, and she looked quite vexed, and not at all disposed to "make the best of it," as she took the chair which her mother pointed out. School-time came very soon after breakfast, and as soon as they rose from the table, Julia hastened to the garden to gather a bouquet for her teacher. There was a beautiful moss rose-bud which she had been watching for several days, and this morning she expected to find it just enough in bloom.

"Miss Seaton will be delighted, I know," said Julia to herself, as she hurried along. "I heard her say, a few days ago, that she thought there was no flower so beautiful as a moss-rose."

But a great disappointment awaited her. The bud had disappeared: some one must have picked it. Julia could hardly help weeping with grief and vexation. "This is a day of misfortunes!" she exclaimed. "I have had nothing but trouble all the morning. I was so pleased to think that I should have that pretty bud for Miss Seaton this morning, and now some one has gone and picked it, just to trouble me. I will not carry any flowers to school, — not one."

This was a foolish resolution, for there were many other kinds of roses, and beautiful flowers of almost every kind in the garden, but Julia had set her heart upon having that one particular bud, and nothing else would satisfy her. She returned to the house in a very ill-humor, and prepared for school.

"Have you a bouquet for your teacher?" asked her mother, who knew that she generally took one with her in the morning.

"I should have had a beautiful one," replied Julia, rather sullenly, "but some one picked my moss rose-bud, which I have been watching for three or four days."

"Do you mean the one on the bush near the summer-house?"

"Yes, mother."

"I picked that one, Julia; I did not know that you were watching it, and I sent it to your grandmother. But why did you not gather some other flowers? There are beautiful cluster roses; I am sure Miss Seaton would be pleased with them."

"I did not want to carry any flowers, if I could not have the moss rose-bud," replied Julia; "and, besides, it is too late now, it is time I was on my way to school;" and with a hasty good-morning to her mother, the little girl hurried away. She felt a little mortified, however, when she saw Annie Wells go up to the teacher with a pretty bunch of cluster roses, and heard Miss Seaton thank her very gratefully, and say that she was particularly glad to have them, as her mother was not well, and was always much pleased with that kind of rose. "I will put them in water to keep them fresh," she added, "and take them home with me this noon."

"Now isn't that provoking?" thought Julia; "our cluster roses are fifty times as handsome as those, and I might have brought a great deal larger bunch."

It was too late to regret it then, however, for just at this moment the bell stopped ringing, and the scholars took their seats, and commenced the business of the day. Julia had no trouble with the morning recitations, for these lessons had all been carefully prepared at home; but her misfortunes commenced again when she took her slate and pencil, and commenced ciphering. It was a new rule, and somehow she could not understand it. To be sure, Miss Seaton had explained it very carefully to the whole class the day before, but this was just after the *long spelling lesson* had been given out; and Julia was so much vexed with the thought of learning so many words, that she had paid little attention to the explanation. She read the rule several times, and tried one sum after another, but they would not come right. Pretty soon she gave up in despair, and looked toward Miss Seaton to see if she was at leisure to help her. "No, there was the class in grammar, and it always took them *forever* to recite," Julia said to herself, impatiently. So as she could not do her sums, she began to draw a picture, and was so much engaged with it that she did not at first notice when the class closed their books and took their seats. Miss Seaton waited a few moments, as she always did, between each recitation, to see if any scholar required her assistance, and then called another class. Just as they were taking their places, Julia recollected her sums, and went to the desk to ask for help.

"You are too late, Julia, the class is waiting; but I will attend to you at recess, if you like," was the reply.

Julia returned to her seat in ill-humor. "I am

not going to lose my recess, or any part of it, just for these sums," she said to herself. But then came the fear of losing her place in the class; and, rather than do that, she concluded to stay in for a few moments after her school-mates had gone out. Miss Seaton attended to her at once; but the little girl was in such a hurry to join her companions, and so impatient and inattentive, that it was very difficult to make her understand the rule.

"I am afraid you do not understand it clearly yet, Julia," said her teacher, kindly, as she turned hastily away.

"I know I don't. I never shall, Miss Seaton; it is *such* a hard rule."

"It is a very simple one, if you would only give your attention," was the reply; "but perhaps you had better go out now."

Julia hardly waited for the permission, but was at the door almost before Miss Seaton had finished speaking. She did not find her companions very easily, for the day was so fine that their teacher had allowed them a longer recess than usual, and they had wandered to a considerable distance from the school-house.

"They must have gone to the woods," said Julia

to herself; "I will go to the entrance and listen, and perhaps I shall hear their voices;" and away she ran. When she paused to listen, she heard no voices, but she could very distinctly hear some one hammering.

"There they are!" she exclaimed; "they are building something,— a new arbor, perhaps,— or they may be putting up a swing. I can follow the sound of the hammer; they work like real carpenters."

Julia ran hastily along, and soon came in sight of the *carpenter*, but he was by no means such a looking person as she had expected to find. A beautiful golden-winged woodpecker was hard at work, making a nest for himself in the stump of an old tree.

Julia clapped her hands with delight. "If there isn't our very woodpecker that had his nest in the old apple-tree near the school-house!" she exclaimed; "I know him *just as well*. I was so sorry when they cut down the old tree the other day. Poor fellow! he is making another nest for himself."

The woodpecker seemed to be pleased to see Julia, and wished to bid her good-morning, or else he was tired of work, and wished to rest himself, by talking a little; for just at this moment he seated himself on a bough, and began his accustomed "wit-a-wit-wit-wit-weat." I do not know that his call was really any different from usual, but it certainly sounded differently to Julia. It seemed to her that he said, "Make the best, make the best of it." She had not thought of her father's motto before that day, but now it came very forcibly to her mind.

"The woodpecker makes the best of it, sure enough," she said; "for when his old nest was destroyed he went right to work to make another. How strange that he should sing me that song! I had quite forgotten about making the best of it."

Julia walked slowly and thoughtfully back to the school-house. She was thinking over the misfortunes of the morning, and she saw plainly that she had not tried to make the best of any of her little troubles. "I will begin now," she said to herself; "I may have more troubles before night, and I will try to make the best of every one of them."

Julia first tried her good resolution in regard to her arithmetic lesson. "It is a troublesome, vexatious rule," she said to herself, as she once more took up the book, "but I am determined to make the best of it." So she gave her whole attention, and was quite surprised to find how soon the difficulties disappeared.

"It was not so very hard, after all," thought she; "I am glad I made the best of it."

Somehow troubles did not seem to come quite so frequently, now that she was watching for them, and had resolved to make the best of them. The history lesson which was given out for the next day was certainly rather long; but then, as Julia said, "It would be foolish to divide it, for there was no other good place to stop, and so they might as well take it, and make the best of it."

Miss Seaton looked a little surprised at hearing this opinion expressed by Julia, but she said it would give her much pleasure if they could take the whole lesson, and all the class agreed to try.

It was really a trial to Julia to find, on her return from school that day, that her little sister had broken the head of her best doll. She was just going to say that it was entirely spoiled, and that she never wanted to see it again, when she remembered what the woodpecker had said to her in the green woods, and her own good resolutions. So she examined dolly's head quite calmly, and said cheerfully, —

"I am glad you broke the back of the head, and not the face, Rosy. I can make her a pretty lace cap, and then she will look almost as well as ever."

Mrs. Meredith was so much pleased to hear Julia speak in this manner, that she kissed her affectionately, and said that dolly should soon have a new head. When evening came again, and Mr. Meredith was in his accustomed seat, ready to attend to Julia and her lessons, he said, smilingly, —

"Have you remembered to make the best of all your little troubles to-day, my daughter?"

"Not of *all* of them, father; I forgot all about it this forenoon, and it seemed to me that I met with all kinds of troubles, but this afternoon I have remembered, and tried to do better." And then Julia told her father about the pretty woodpecker, and what he seemed to say to her, and Mr. Meredith listened with much interest; and when Julia asked him if it was not strange that the bird should seem to say, "Make the best of it," he told her that the good spirits, who were trying to help her to do right, put it into her mind that the bird said these words, in order to remind her of the advice he had given her the evening before.

Julia understood this very well, for she knew that the good spirits were always trying to help her to do right; but still she loved to think that the woodpecker had really said those words, and that night she dreamed that she again saw him perched upon the bough, and calling out to her in a very cheerful voice, which sounded extremely like her father's, "Make the best of it."

ISABEL'S BIRTHDAY.

"WHAT an odd little figure!" exclaimed Isabel Crawford, one of a merry party of school-girls, who, with baskets and tin boxes in their hands, were roaming through the woods and fields, one delightful summer afternoon, in search of flowers to arrange in their herbariums.

Isabel's companions looked in the direction to which she pointed, and echoed her exclamation as they saw a little girl with a sun-bonnet almost as large as herself upon her head, and a cape upon her shoulders, extending nearly to her naked feet.

"She may be one of the fairies that we love so much to read about," suggested a bright-eyed little miss among the group.

Her remark was received with shouts of laughter from her companions.

"A fairy indeed! Oh Rosalie, what an idea! She looks more like an orang-outang!"

"No; like a mushroom," remarked Isabel, as the child stooped down among the bushes, after a hasty glance at the party, and resumed her occupation of picking the ripe blueberries with which the fields abounded. "But we will not laugh at her, girls, it is not right. She may be a very good child, if she is an odd figure. Dress does not make the man, you know."

"How wise Isabel is growing!" laughingly observed one of the girls. "I expect she will soon wear a cap and spectacles."

"Not quite yet, Miss Kate," returned Isabel good-humoredly. "To confess the truth, the teacher gave me that little sentence for a copy to-day. But I know it is true; and so I am going to have a talk with that little lady yonder, and find out what kind of a head and heart live under the shelter of that great cape and bonnet."

As Isabel said this, she walked hastily toward the little berry-girl, followed by several of her companions.

The child looked up timidly as they approached, and seemed half inclined to run away; but Isabel's smiling countenance and kind words soon reassured her, and she picked away as industriously as ever.

"What a large pail of berries you have gathered!" said Isabel. "Are you going to sell any of them? or will you and your brothers and sisters eat them for your supper?"

"Oh! I have no brothers and sisters, miss," replied the little girl. "Mother and I live all alone in that little cottage at the foot of the hill. You can just see the chimney from here. I am going to sell the berries in the village. I sold four quarts yesterday, and to-day I shall have six or eight to sell. Mother will be very glad."

"Do you give all the money to your mother?" asked Isabel.

"Yes, indeed, miss; she needs it all very much. She used to sew a great deal, and then we had all we wanted; but she grew so sick and weak, that the doctor said she must not sew any more. Then we grew very poor, and at last we had to sell our cow. Oh! I was very sorry then; for I loved poor Mooly so much. I could milk her myself, she was so gentle. But mother said it would be wrong to keep her when we had not enough to give her to eat. Before my father died, she gave a great deal of milk; and we used to sell it to the neighbors, and that helped us along very much; but when we grew poor, and could not feed her well, she gave very little milk; so we had none to sell. I was afraid we should never have any more money when mother took all that Farmer Jennings gave her for the cow, and paid the grocer and the doctor; but she said it was right to pay them, and that the Lord would take care of us, for He takes care of even the little sparrows. And now I know that He does take care of us, for He has made all these nice berries to grow, and I shall pick them and sell them, and earn a great deal of money for my mother."

The tears came to Isabel's eyes as she listened to the simple story of the little berry-girl. She was the only child of wealthy parents, who delighted to do everything for her comfort and happiness; and it seemed to her very strange and sad that there were people so poor as to be thankful for the little money they could earn by picking berries.

"What is your name, little girl?" she asked, as the child paused in her story.

"Jenny, miss,—Jenny Green," was the reply.

And Jenny got up from the grass where she had been kneeling, and dropped her little courtesy, as her mother had taught her to do when any one inquired her name.

Isabel's companions smiled; but she looked very serious as she said, "Well, little girl, if you will bring your berries to our house at six o'clock, we will buy them all, and my mamma will give you some tea and sugar for your sick mother. Do you know where Mr. Crawford lives?"

How Jenny's eyes sparkled, as she replied, "Oh, yes, miss, — in the great white house with the beautiful garden! I will bring the berries. And, oh, my mother will be so glad to have a cup of tea! She never buys any now; but it always made her feel better when she was sick and tired."

"Very well, Jenny; she shall have a nice cup this evening," said Isabel, her eyes still glistening with tears. "Do not forget to come at six; I will be at home then. Good-by for the present!"

"She *is* a nice little girl, Isabel!" exclaimed Kate Barton, as they walked away. "I give you great credit for discovering her good qualities. How much she loves her mother! She seems to have no thought for herself."

"The few shillings that she can earn by picking berries will do very little toward their support," remarked Isabel, thoughtfully. "Something must be done for them."

"There are a great many poor people in the neighborhood," returned Kate. "My mother gave away such a heap of old clothes the other day!"

"But I want to do something for them *myself*," replied Isabel. "My father and mother do a great deal for the poor; but they have often told me that I must not think that this is the same as if I did it myself."

"But how *can* you do anything?" argued Kate. "If you give away money, or food, or clothing, it is not really giving what is your own; for everything that we have belongs to our parents."

"That is very true," replied Isabel. "But yet there are some ways in which we can help the poor. We can often read to them, and teach them many things; and although we have no money that is really our own, yet, if we desire it, our parents are sometimes willing to allow us to give up some pleasure which they have promised us, and use the money in helping others."

"I do not understand exactly what you mean," said Kate, with a puzzled air.

"I will explain it to you," replied Isabel. "Last winter, my father had promised me a new beaver hat; but, before he purchased it, old Susan's cottage was burned to the ground, and I wanted very much to do something to help her. So I asked my father, if I would wear my old hat all winter, whether he would give me the money that a new one would cost to buy clothes for Susan. He was quite willing; and mother helped me to buy the clothes and make them."

"Well, Isabel, you are a strange girl!" exclaimed Kate, with a merry laugh. "If my father was as rich as yours, I would have had the beaver hat, and the money for Susan besides."

"But there would have been no self-denial in that, Kate. The money would not have been mine to give."

"I do not see much difference in either case," replied Kate; "and I should not care anything about it, so long as the poor did not suffer. It is just as well for them to receive help from our parents as from us."

"But not so well for us, Kate."

"Perhaps not; but I am not so much of a philosopher as you are, Isabel. And as for the self-denial that you speak of,—I never had much fancy for it. I like to enjoy myself while I can. I wonder what scheme you will hit upon to buy another cow for that poor woman? You will have to go without any new clothing next winter."

"Not quite so bad as that, I hope," replied Isabel, with a quiet smile. "But come, Kate; the girls are far ahead of us. Let us try to overtake them; and then we will all sit down upon the rocks around our favorite brook, and arrange our flowers."

"Agreed," answered Kate. "Now for a race! I can beat you at that, Miss Isabel; although you have the advantage of me in reasoning."

"Run for your life, then!" was Isabel's laughing reply. And away scampered the two girls across the green fields, regardless of bushes and briers, until, out of breath, they joined their companions, who were quietly standing to watch the race.

Just as the clock in the village church struck six, little Jenny Green stood at the door of Mr. Crawford's handsome mansion. Isabel had not forgotten her promise to be ready for her at that hour. She had told the story to her mother, and received permission to buy the berries, and to give Jenny several articles of suitable clothing. Mrs. Crawford had packed a small basket of provisions, and had advised Isabel to go herself to the cottage, as she would then be better able to judge of the truth of what Jenny had told her, and could also make more particular inquiries into the wants of the poor woman.

Jenny appeared much delighted when she found that her new friend intended to accompany her home.

She trudged merrily along, with the heavy basket in one hand, and the empty pail in the other, declining all Isabel's offers of assistance, until at length they stood at the door of a small but very neat-looking cottage at the foot of a hill, so steep that it almost deserved the title of a mountain.

"The young lady has come to see you, mother!" exclaimed Jenny, as she opened the cottage-door, and invited Isabel to walk in.

"She is very kind," replied a pleasant voice; and Mrs. Green came forward to welcome her visitor.

She was neatly dressed, and had a cheerful, contented expression of countenance; although she looked pale and feeble, as though she had been very ill.

Isabel inquired kindly concerning her health; and she replied that she was much better, and hoped soon to be able to work again.

"You will not have to work for a long time, dear mother," said Jenny. "Just look at this great basket of nice things that the young lady's mother has sent you! and see all the money that she paid me for my berries! Before you have spent all this, I shall have earned some more. Oh, how I wish I could earn enough to buy a cow! Then you could sell the milk again, and we should have all we wanted."

Mrs. Green smiled.

"You forget that the cow must be fed, Jenny," she said. "But do not trouble the young lady with all our griefs. There is a beautiful rose-bud upon your bush; would you not like to give it to her?"

"Oh, yes, very much!" exclaimed Jenny; and she ran to her little garden, and soon returned with the bud.

"My dear father planted the rose-bush for me," she said; "and there are roses upon it every month."

"It is very beautiful," said Isabel, as she took the bud. "I will put it in water as soon as I get home, Jenny, and it will be fresh and sweet for many days; and to-morrow, when you bring us some more berries, I will give you a sprig of my monthly honeysuckle." Jenny's eyes sparkled with pleasure as she heard this, and Mrs. Green thanked Isabel for her kindness to the little girl.

"She tries to be a good child," she said, "and she is a great comfort to me. She has worked very hard since I have been ill; but, as soon as I am a little stronger, I shall try to let her go to school again."

"Can you read, Jenny?" asked Isabel.

"Oh, yes, miss! I can read a chapter in the Bible without missing one word. And I have three little story-books that my teacher gave me; I can read them pretty well."

Isabel thought that she would give Jenny some of her old story-books when she came the next day; but she did not say anything about it then, as she had not consulted her mother. She bade

Mrs. Green and Jenny good-by, and promised to come to the cottage again before many days. Then she walked slowly toward home, thinking over many plans for doing good to the widow and her little girl.

For several days Jenny continued to bring her fresh berries to Mr. Crawford's, and received many little gifts from Isabel and her mother. Mrs. Crawford also visited the cottage with Isabel, and was so much pleased with Mrs. Green that she sent her own physician to see her, and provided her with many comforts.

Mr. Crawford would frequently inquire with interest for Isabel's "little berry-girl;" and he had promised that a barrel of apples, and a good supply of winter vegetables, should be sent to the cottage after the harvest.

Mrs. Green's health improved very much, and she was soon able to do many things to aid in their support, although too close attention to needle-work brought on a return of her old complaints.

Isabel had now nearly reached her twelfth birthday. Her father had promised her a party, and the event was already much talked of among her companions; for, as we have already said, she was an only child, and her parents were wealthy, and loved to do everything to promote her happiness. There was to be music and dancing, and an elegant supper, and everything else that could be desired, at the birthday party; and Isabel looked forward to it with great anticipations of delight.

"You had better have your little berry-girl for one of the waiters at your party, Isabel," said Mr. Crawford, as they were talking over the arrangements one evening, "She will be useful to you, and it will give her pleasure to see all that is going on."

"Thank you, father," replied Isabel. "Jenny will be delighted to come, I am sure."

"How does she get along with her studies?" asked Mr. Crawford. "Your mother tells me that you are teaching her arithmetic."

"She learns very fast, father. Her mother will send her to school next winter, if she is well enough to spare her."

"Mrs. Green is quite strong again now; is she not, Isabel?"

"Much better than she was; but the sewing still gives her the bad pain in her side. I wish she had something else to do. When they had a cow she used to sell milk and fresh butter, and this brought them in a good deal of money; but, while Mrs. Green was ill, they grew so poor that the cow had to be sold to pay their debts."

"That was a pity," returned Mr. Crawford. "A cow is a great blessing to a poor person; that is, if they have enough to feed one."

"But they had not, father; that was one great trouble. Jenny could pasture the cow at the sides of the road during the summer; but in the winter they needed hay for her, and they had no money to buy it."

"I would willingly have given them the hay if I had known the circumstances, and then they need not have parted with the cow," replied Mr. Crawford.

"I wish they had another, father," said Isabel, earnestly. "Do you not think you could afford to buy them one?"

"I hardly think I can," answered her father, stroking her hair affectionately. "We people who are called rich have a great many ways to spend our money. There is my little daughter's party, for instance: that will cost me as much as a cow. I will try to help Mrs. Green through the winter; but I do not think I can afford to give them so large a sum."

Isabel was silent, and seemed to be thinking deeply.

"You must not be grieved at my refusal, my child," said her father. "You know that I would gladly oblige you, if I thought it would be right."

"I know that, father; I am not grieved," replied Isabel; but still she remained very thoughtful.

After a long silence, she said, "Father, if I will give up my party, will you buy a cow for Mrs. Green?"

"Give up your party, my dear Isabel! Can you make up your mind to do this, when you have looked forward to it so long?"

"Not very easily, father; but I think I *can* do it. The pleasure that we should have from the party seems of little consequence, when I think of the good that the money would do Mrs. Green."

It was now Mr. Crawford's turn to be silent and thoughtful. At length he said, "I will speak to your mother about it, Isabel; and to-morrow morning we will talk on the subject again. Perhaps you will repent of a too hasty decision."

Both Mr. and Mrs. Crawford felt a little reluctance at the thought of Isabel's giving up her party; and at one time her father half resolved to buy the cow himself, and not ask for any sacrifice on her part. But her mother opposed this course; for she felt sure that the self-denial would be good for Isabel, and she did not think it would be right for them to deprive her of this good.

"We will let her take her own course," she said to her husband. "She will lose her party, it is true; but the act of kindness will bring around her many good and gentle spirits, and she will be happier than with her earthly companions."

When Isabel came to her father in the morning, therefore, and told him that she still wished to buy the cow, he consented at once, and promised that he would attend to the business himself, and would see that she was provided with food for the first year at least.

When Isabel's companions questioned her, as usual, about the expected party, she felt a little at a loss what to say to them. She could easily tell them that she had concluded not to have it; but then they would want a reason, and she was unwilling to speak of her generosity to Mrs. Green.

Kate Barton, however, suspected at once that her friend had denied herself the expected pleasure for some purpose of charity; and begged so earnestly to know all about it, that Isabel told her the whole truth.

Kate, and indeed all the girls, were a good deal disappointed at first; but many of them had become quite interested in little Jenny and her mother, and they could not help rejoicing that they were to receive so valuable a gift.

And now Kate Barton appeared to have some little secret of her own. She had called at Mr. Crawford's one afternoon, when she well knew that Isabel was absent, and had quite a long talk with her mother. After this, there was a good deal of whispering and consultation among the elder girls at the school; and finally Isabel was told that they had concluded to celebrate the afternoon of her birthday by having a little picnic, and invited her to join them.

"We are going to the grove near Mrs. Green's cottage," said Kate. "You know what a pleasant place it is, Isabel. It has been nicely cleared up within a few days, and is all ready for a picnic."

Isabel entered readily into the plans of her

school-mates, and promised to be early on the picnic ground, and to bring an abundance of flowers to decorate the table.

"How I wish father could have bought the cow before the picnic!" said Isabel to her mother, as she told her of the proposed pleasure; "then Mrs. Green could have treated us to some fresh milk, and Jenny would have felt so proud and happy. But father is very busy at present, and he says I must not hurry him, for he must take his own time for such an important purchase."

"Very true," replied Mrs. Crawford, smiling. "Do not hurry him, Isabel; the cow will come in good time. I am much pleased with the kindness of your companions in celebrating your birthday, and I have no doubt you will all have a happy afternoon."

"I hope the weather will be pleasant," said Isabel; and her hope was not disappointed. The day appointed for the picnic was one of the most lovely of all the autumn days, and the faces of the happy party in the grove were as cloudless as the sky.

"First of all, we must choose our queen!" exclaimed Kate Barton, when all the girls had assembled, and kindly greetings had passed between them.

"She is already chosen, is she not?" remarked one of the other girls. "We have only to crown her, and conduct her to the throne."

"Very true," replied Kate; "and here is the crown," she added, producing a beautiful wreath of autumnal leaves and flowers, and placing it upon Isabel's head.

"Long live Queen Isabel!" exclaimed many voices, as Kate took the hand of the new-made queen, and led her to a mossy seat, which was to serve the purpose of a throne.

Isabel was so much astonished at this unexpected honor, that she found it difficult to recover her self-possession sufficiently to reply in a dignified and proper manner to the congratulations of her subjects, and to receive the numerous gifts of flowers and fruit which were now presented to her.

Just as she was becoming more at ease in her new position, Jenny, the little berry-girl, appeared, bearing in her hand a small but beautifully chased silver cup, and with her usual modest courtesy, presented it to the queen.

"The speech, the speech!" urged Kate, laying her hand gently upon the little girl's shoulder.

Jenny looked up with a bewildered air.

"I cannot, Miss Kate. Indeed, I tried to remember it, and I have just said it every word to my mother; but now it has all gone out of my mind. I can only say, dear Miss Isabel, I love you, and thank you with all my heart."

Here Jenny's voice failed her, and she burst into tears. The queen, and several of her subjects, appeared much disposed to follow her example. Even the gay Kate brushed the drops from her eyes as she exclaimed, "Was there ever anything so provoking! — that eloquent speech that I have taken so much pains to prepare! But will your majesty be pleased to taste the contents of your cup?" she continued, playfully addressing Isabel, who still held the cup in her hand, apparently quite unconscious of what it contained.

Isabel started, and raised the cup to her lips.

"Milk! warm new milk!" she exclaimed, springing from the throne. "The cow has come at last!"

"Yes, miss, she has come," said Jenny, smiling through her tears. "And such a beauty you never saw; and so gentle, that I can milk her just as easily as I could our old one. But you have not looked at the beautiful cup, Miss Isabel."

Ashamed of her neglect of the costly gift of her companions, Isabel hastened to examine it, and, with the tears still gathering in her eyes, read the simple inscription, — "ISABEL: from her Affectionate School-mates."

"It is beautiful, and I do thank you very much," she said earnestly, as she looked around upon them all; "but, like Jenny, I cannot make any speech."

"We do not want any," replied Kate. "You have said enough. There shall be no speeches to-day, since the one that I planned has failed. And now, girls, let us pay our respects to Jenny's new treasure. I saw her quietly feeding in the field near the cottage."

Away ran all the girls; and, in spite of Kate's boasted fleetness, Isabel was the first to reach the field; for her impatience to see the cow seemed to give her wings.

The cow looked somewhat astonished at the merry group, and greeted them with a low "Moo-oo!" as if to inquire their business; but, finding that they had no intention of molesting her, she quietly went on feeding as before.

She was a fine-looking animal; and, after sufficiently admiring her, the girls went to the cottage to wish Mrs. Green joy, and to get the large pail of milk which Jenny assured them was ready for their suppers.

The table in the grove was soon beautifully spread; and the girls joyfully welcomed Mr. and Mrs. Crawford, and several other ladies and gentlemen, who had walked that way to witness the scene.

All seemed to enjoy the feast, and the milk was pronounced to be of a very superior quality.

Many a merry game was played, and many a sweet song sung, before the twilight reminded them that it was time to seek their own homes.

It had been a happy afternoon, and one which none of the little party would soon forget. In after years, when looking back upon their pleasant school-days, one of the most cherished reminiscences was that of the picnic on Isabel's birthday.

"I'LL TELL MOTHER."

"I'LL tell mother!" exclaimed Georgie Benton. "I'll go and tell her this very moment."

Georgie was at play in the pleasant yard with his two brothers, John and Oscar, and his little sister Kate. John had taken Georgie's hoop from its nail in the wood-shed, and was trundling it up and down the pathway with great delight. Georgie had been very happy, blowing soap-bubbles to amuse little Kate; but, when he saw John with the hoop, he claimed it at once, and told his brother to hang it up again immediately. Johnny was not disposed to obey; and, as Georgie had been taught not to use force, he resolved to go and complain to his mother.

Mrs. Benton was very busy with her sewing; but she looked up pleasantly as Georgie entered, and said, "Well, Georgie, what is it? Is Kate tired of the bubbles?"

"No, mother; she likes them very much: but John has got my hoop."

"Do you want to use it now, George?"

"No, mother; but I do not like to have him take my things without my leave."

"He ought not to do so, Georgie; but you know he is not so old as you, and has not learned so well what is right."

"May I tell him that you say he must hang it up in its place?" asked George.

"Is he injuring it, George?"

"I don't know, mother; but I want him to hang it up."

"Very well, you may tell him that I say he must hang up the hoop, and come to me."

Georgie returned to the yard in triumph.

"There, Johnny!" he exclaimed, "I told mother, and she says you must hang up the hoop, and come to her."

Johnny obeyed; but he looked unhappy, and walked towards the house with slow, unwilling steps. Very soon, however, he returned with his face all smiles and sunshine again.

"Georgie," he said pleasantly, "will you please to lend me your hoop a little while? I will be very careful of it."

George could not refuse, although there was a little selfishness in his heart, which made him somewhat unwilling to say "Yes," even now that the request had been made in a proper manner.

He, however, consented; and Johnny joyfully took possession of the desired plaything.

For about ten minutes the children played very happily. Georgie blew the bright-colored bubbles; Kate clapped her hands, and tried to catch them as they rose in the air; Johnny rolled the hoop up and down the path; and Oscar was very busy digging in his little garden.

But pretty soon the words, "I'll tell mother," were again heard. Georgie had mischievously directed some of his bubbles toward Oscar, as the little boy kneeled by his garden; and two or three of them had burst upon his head and his rosy cheeks.

So mother had to be told; and a message came to Georgie that he "must not do so; for it was not right."

Georgie smiled, and turned his pipe in another

direction; and Oscar went on with his work: but, as he was now digging on the side of his garden nearest to the path, he was in the way of Johnny's hoop; and several times it hit against him, and was turned out of its course, and fell to the ground. Johnny did not like this; and, as Oscar refused to move, he marched off to the house to "tell mother."

I do not know what message would have been sent to Oscar; for, just after Johnny went with his complaint, little Kate, — whose heart had been made very glad by the beautiful bubbles that Georgie had blown for her, by a flower which Oscar had given to her, and by having been allowed by Johnny to drive the hoop several times around the yard, — suddenly clapped her little hands, exclaiming, —

"Now *I'll* tell mother: *I'll* tell her about Georgie, and about Oscar, and about Johnny." And away she ran, so fast that Georgie followed her, fearing that she would fall. Oscar did not wish to stay alone; and, besides, he felt curious to know what Kate had to tell: so he also went into the house; and, in a few moments, all the children were in their mother's room.

Johnny had finished his story when the others entered. Little Kate ran up to her mother, and, putting up her mouth for a kiss, exclaimed,—

"*I've* come to tell you, too, mamma. I'll tell you that Georgie is a good boy: he blows pretty bubbles. Oscar is a good boy: he gave me this flower. And Johnny is a good boy, and let me drive his hoop."

"And Kate is a darling good little girl, and has made mamma glad by telling her such a pretty story," said their mother, as she stooped to kiss the little pet.

The three boys looked a little ashamed, and their mother said to them kindly,—

"Perhaps you have never thought, my dear children, how much it troubles me to have you come every few minutes with some little unpleasant tale. If there is any serious difficulty between you, it is certainly right to come to me to settle it; but if you try to be yielding, and kind to each other, you may play together as happily as those little lambs that we saw the other day frisking in the green meadow. Try to follow Kate's example, and 'tell mother' of all the pleasant things that happen. This will make you happy: and it will make me happy also; for little acts of kindness among children are like sunbeams to their mother's heart."

THE CHRISTMAS GIFTS.

"OH EMILY!" exclaimed Rose Grant, as she bounded into the room where her sister was seated at the piano, carefully practising her last lesson, "I am so sorry that you did not stop after school with the rest of the girls! We called and called after you, but you would not stop to listen,—only turn, and shake your head."

"Because, if I had stopped to listen, you would, perhaps, have persuaded me to stay; and I knew that it was my duty to come home, and attend to my music," replied Emily, looking up at her sister with a pleasant smile.

"You always talk about *duty*," returned Rose. "But never mind; I will tell you what we had a meeting for, and you can join us just as well as if you had been there."

"Please tell me by and by, Rose, because I want to practise as much as possible before dark, and you know the days are so short now, that we have very little time after school."

"Oh! it will take me but a few minutes to tell you, and you will have plenty of time to practise," persisted Rose; but, just then, her mother's voice was heard from the next room, —

"Do not interrupt your sister, Rose. Put your hat and cloak in their proper place, and then come to me."

Rose reluctantly obeyed, and Emily saw no more of her until it was too dark to distinguish the notes of her music. Then the piano was closed; and, in a few moments, the two sisters were conversing earnestly together in their own little room.

"We have such a nice plan for Christmas!" said Rose. "We are all going to join together, and make the teacher a beautiful present."

"What are you going to give him?" asked Emily.

"A Bible, — a beautiful Bible; elegantly bound, with handsome clasps. It will cost a good many dollars; but then there are a good many of us to buy it; so it will not be difficult to make up the money. Every one is to give what they like. Some of the girls will only give twenty-five cents; but I would not be so mean as that. I put my name down for a dollar, and so did almost all the girls in our class."

"But a dollar is half of what you have saved for Christmas gifts," replied Emily. "If you give so much toward our teacher's present, you will have very little for your other friends."

"I know that," answered Rose; "and I am very sorry; but what could I do? I did not like to give less than the other girls."

"Our parents are not wealthy," said Emily, "and we cannot afford to give so much as some others. Indeed, I do not think that I can afford to give anything toward the Bible."

"Not give anything!" exclaimed Rose. "Oh Emily! I never thought you could be so stingy. Not give anything to our teacher, who is always so kind to us?"

"I did not say I would not give him anything, Rosie," replied her sister, smiling good-naturedly; "I only said that I did not think I could give anything toward the Bible. I have made a very pretty pen-wiper for our teacher; for I notice that he needs a new one on his desk. I do not mean to be *stingy*, as you call it; but I have but two dollars to spend, and there are several things that I want to buy."

"But you could do without them, Emily," eagerly urged Rose. "You are so handy, you know, that you can always make all sorts of things out of almost nothing. I am sure you have got a great box full of needle-books and pin-cushions, and pen-wipers and collars, and all sorts of things, for Christmas gifts; so you can give a dollar toward the Bible just as well as not."

Emily shook her head. "There are some persons who must have a different kind of Christmas gift from anything in my box, Rosie," she said. "But never mind; there are enough of you to buy the Bible, even if I do not join you."

"Oh, yes, there are enough of us to be sure; but I shall feel so mortified if you refuse to join us. And what will the teacher think, when he reads the note that we are going to send him with the Bible, and does not see your name down? He will suppose that you do not care anything about him."

"But you forget my pen-wiper," returned Emily, smiling at her sister's look of mortification. "That will at least show him that I have not forgotten him in my Christmas gifts. But we will not talk any more about it now, Rosie. I must go, and have a frolic with baby before tea; and you can amuse George and Willie. Mother will be glad of our help, I am sure."

The days passed swiftly by, and Christmas came almost too quickly for those who had a good many little gifts to prepare; but the children were all ready for it, as usual; and "a merry Christmas, a merry Christmas!" was heard from hundreds of cheerful little voices. We hope that all these happy little ones remembered that there were many to whom this Christmas could not be a merry one, and that they were willing to share their blessings with those who were less happy than they.

The Bible, with its elegant binding and handsome clasps, had been purchased; and the note to the teacher, begging his acceptance of the gift, had been written, with the names of the girls from whom it came, each in her own handwriting. Much to the chagrin of Rose, Emily had persisted in her refusal to join them. Rose had begged her mother to advise her to do so; but Mrs. Grant said that she would rather allow Emily to act in freedom in the case.

Emily had presented her pen-wiper to her teacher on the day before Christmas, and he had seemed much pleased with it. He had also received some other trifling gifts, principally from the younger children. The Bible was to be taken to his own house, on Christmas morning, by three of the girls, who were chosen by the others to present the gift. Rose was one of the three; and, as she was leaving the house on Christmas morning to meet her young companions, she could not help saying to Emily, —

"Ah! Emily, do you not wish that you were going with me?"

"No," replied her sister, pleasantly; "I have had one good walk this morning."

"Oh, yes! I know you have been to carry some clothing and food to poor people; but don't you wish that you were going with us to present our beautiful Bible?"

"I *have* presented a Bible this morning, already," answered Emily, smiling.

"A Bible!" exclaimed Rose, in great surprise;

but, at this instant, the door-bell rang, and the voices of her school-mates were heard. They had called for her on their way to the teacher's house; and Rose joined them immediately, although her sister's words had filled her with curiosity.

"To whom can she have presented a Bible?" she said to herself. "I am sure it was not to father or mother; for I saw the gifts for them. I do wish I knew! I will ask her the moment that I go home."

The walk was not a long one; and the girls were soon at their teacher's door, and were preparing to ring, when a pleasant voice behind them wished them a "happy Christmas"; and, on turning around, they saw the teacher himself.

"You are most welcome, young ladies," he said, kindly. "Allow me to open the door for you. I am very glad that I returned in season to enjoy your morning call."

As he said this, he opened the door, and led the way into a pleasant room which he called his study. Here the beautiful gift was presented, and very gratefully accepted.

"My pupils could not have presented me with any gift which I should value so highly," said their teacher; "and I shall often read this pleasant note, and think of those who have so kindly remembered me."

As he said this, Rose thought of her sister, and wished more than ever that her name could have been affixed to the note.

"This is the second agreeable surprise that I have received this morning," continued their teacher. "I have just returned from visiting several poor families in the neighborhood. One old woman among them is so generally known, that I dare say you have all heard of her. 'Nurse Whiting,' she is usually called."

"Yes sir, I know her!" and "I know her!" exclaimed the girls.

"We often go to see her," said Rosie. "Emily went this morning, and carried her some flannel, and a new cap, that mother sent her for Christmas."

"Was that all, Miss Rose? Do you not know of your sister's own Christmas gift to the good old woman?"

"No sir," replied Rosie, blushing deeply; for she felt a little mortified that she *did not* know.

"Then I will go on with my story," continued the teacher.

"I had some little comforts for the poor people; but, as I walked along, I was thinking of one most appropriate gift for Nurse Whiting, and I was considering whether my duty to my own family would allow me to purchase it for her. This was a copy of the Word, with very large, clear type, suitable for the declining sight of the old woman. I knew that she dearly loved to read in the Word of the Lord; and I had heard her regret that her sight was failing, so that it was becoming difficult for her to use her well-worn Bible.

"When I reached Nurse Whiting's room, and presented my little gift, — which was only some few comfortable things for her Christmas dinner, — she thanked me with tears in her eyes, and said that the Lord had indeed been mindful of her that morning; for He had sent her the very thing that she most wished for. She then showed me a large, neatly bound Bible, with most excellent type, which she said had just been presented to her by one of my scholars. I was so much pleased to hear this, that I turned immediately to the blank leaf, where I found your sister's name, Miss

Rose, very neatly written in her own handwriting.

"'Only read what it says!' exclaimed the delighted old woman: 'Nurse Whiting, from her young friend Emily Grant. How many times I shall read those words, and pray for God's blessing upon her!' The tears streamed down her cheeks as she said this; and I must confess that my own eyes filled with tears, but they were tears of pleasure to think that one of my pupils should have done so kind and thoughtful an act. And now, young ladies, as I have finished my story, I will write a little note of thanks to the kind young friends who have so generously remembered me; and, in the mean time, please to amuse yourselves with looking over my books and engravings."

The girls found abundant amusement upon the neat centre-table, and were almost sorry when their teacher returned to them.

"Here is my note," he said; "and here is another, Miss Rose, which you will please to hand to your sister. I could not refrain from writing a few words to thank her for the great pleasure she has given me this morning."

Rose hardly knew whether to laugh or cry, as she handed the note to her sister.

"The teacher liked our gift very much," she said, in answer to her mother's inquiries; "but I really believe he thought more of the Bible which Emily gave to Nurse Whiting than he did of his own; and he has written a note to thank her for it. I think Emily might have told me what she intended to do with her money."

"Do you honestly think that it would have made any difference in your own plans, Rose?" asked her mother.

"I do not think it would, mother," answered Rose, reluctantly.

"Then put away that little feeling of envy from your heart, Rose; or, perhaps I should say, of jealousy of your teacher's praise of your sister; and go and put your arms around her neck, and tell her that you will not think her stingy another time."

"I did not *really* think her so," replied Rose, smiling, as she gave her sister a hearty embrace; "only I was afraid that the *teacher* would think her so."

"And now you are very glad to find that he does not," said Emily, returning the embrace; "and I am glad too: so now come to our room, and get ready for our Christmas party."

GOING DOWN HILL.

"WHO is that boy to whom you were speaking just now, Willie?" asked Uncle George, as he stood with his little nephew upon the summit of a high hill, which they had climbed in order to obtain a favorable view of the surrounding country.

"That was Rufus Lyman, uncle," replied Willie. "But I was not speaking to him exactly. I only said two or three words, just for fun, to make him go away."

"Rufus Lyman!" exclaimed Uncle George. "Not Widow Lyman's son, surely? He used to be a fine-looking lad."

"This is the same boy, uncle. He has changed very much, of late. We never play with him now, and seldom speak to him. He is always loafing around, and does not come to school, or play on the village green, as he used to do. People say that he is getting to be a very bad boy; and I think so myself." And Willie drew himself up with an air of importance as he pronounced the last words.

"Poor boy!" said Uncle George. "I am sorry to hear so bad an account of him. His father was a very worthy man; and his mother is a good woman, and must feel much grieved to see her son going down hill in this manner."

"Going down hill, uncle!" repeated Willie. "I do not understand what you mean."

"When we see a person becoming poorer or more wicked, or changing for the worse in any way," replied his uncle, "we often say that he is 'going down hill.' We mean that he is sinking from a higher state to a lower one."

"Yes, uncle; I understand you now. Rufus is going down hill fast enough, I am sure."

"And I suppose a great many of you give him a little push occasionally, so as to make him go down a little faster; do you not?" asked his uncle.

"Why, uncle, what a strange question!" exclaimed Willie.

"Not at all, Willie. I have seen a great many men, who, either from want of feeling or want of thought, would give a strong push to some poor unfortunate person whom they saw going in the downward path; and I have no doubt it is much the same with boys. Are there any among you who treat Rufus in a friendly manner, or try to do him any good?"

Willie hung his head; but he was an honest boy, and he answered frankly,—

"No uncle; we all laugh at him, and tease him whenever he comes in our way."

"And this makes him worse, Willie, and sends him down hill faster than he would otherwise go. Now, supposing I should slip from this rock, and roll down the steep bank, should you run after me, and push me to make me roll down faster?"

"No, indeed, uncle. I should try to stop you, and help you up again."

"I have no doubt you would, Willie. And this is exactly what you ought to try to do for poor Rufus. Do not push him down lower and lower, but try to help him up again."

"But I do not know how, uncle."

"Try, my boy. It may not be so difficult as you imagine. Leave off trying to vex him, and endeavor to make him see that you wish to be his friend; it will then be easier to find some way in which you can do him good. Do you know why he no longer attends school?"

"I suppose he is ashamed to come in those ragged clothes," replied Willie, thoughtfully. "I never thought much about it before; but I dare say his mother is too poor to buy him good clothes. I know she has been sick a great deal since Mr. Lyman died. I am sorry that I called Rufus 'Old Clothesman;' for my own clothes would be no better than his, if I had no one to buy me any."

"That is very true, Willie. I see that you are beginning to think rightly on the subject," answered his uncle. "I have no doubt you can do Rufus much good; and, if I can help you in any way, you must let me know."

"Yes sir, I will," returned Willie. And, as they walked toward home, his mind was filled with busy thoughts concerning Rufus; and he formed many plans for placing himself upon a more friendly footing with him.

When we really desire to do good to others, the opportunity is seldom wanting. On the day following the conversation with his uncle, as Willie was returning from school, he saw Rufus in a field adjoining the road, endeavoring to pick up a large quantity of blackberries which lay spilled upon the grass.

"I will help him," thought Willie. And, springing over the fence, he said, in a friendly tone, —

"Have you spilled your berries, Rufus? Never mind; the grass is clean, and we can easily gather them up. What fine large berries! Are you going to take them to your mother?"

Rufus was so much surprised at Willie's friendly manner, that he did not reply for a few moments, but at length he said, hesitatingly, —

"I was going to try to sell them."

"Well, you will get a good price for them, I am sure," returned Willie. "I have no doubt my mother would buy them; she often buys blackberries. Come home with me, and I will ask her."

Rufus made little reply to this proposal of Willie's; but, after the berries were replaced in the basket, he silently followed him home.

Willie carried the berries to his mother, and soon returned with the money, which he handed to Rufus, saying,—

"Mother says if you can bring her ten quarts of berries as good as these, she should be glad to buy them to preserve for winter."

"I will bring them to-morrow afternoon, or the next day, at farthest," replied Rufus, looking much pleased. And, as he turned to go away, he looked back, and said, "Thank you, Willie."

"He will like me now," thought Willie, as he returned to the house. "How pleasant his voice sounded when he said 'Thank you, Willie!' I do not believe he wants to be a bad boy. To-morrow I will ask him why he does not come to school."

Rufus was certainly not an *idle* boy; for, on the following afternoon, he brought to Willie's mother ten quarts of large ripe blackberries, all of which he had picked with his own hands since early morning.

After he had received his pay, Willie walked along with him in the direction of his own home.

"Why don't you come to school now, Rufus?" he asked in a kind tone, after they had talked for some minutes upon different subjects.

"I have no clothes that are fit to wear," replied Rufus in a low voice, looking down, at the same time, upon his patched garments.

"Never mind your clothes," answered Willie. "You can study, even if your clothes are not good."

"But the boys all laugh at me," returned Rufus; "and then I grow angry and wicked. My mother would rather have me stay at home than feel so."

"I am sorry that I have ever laughed at you, Rufus; I never will again. Do come to school; and, if the boys tease you, try to be patient, and they will soon leave it off."

Rufus shook his head; but Willie continued, —

"Remember what a good scholar you used to be, Rufus. You were the best reader in our class."

"It is all different now," answered Rufus; and his voice trembled, as if it were very difficult for him to keep from crying. "When my dear father lived with us, I was a better boy than I am now; and I loved to go to school, and to learn to do many useful things. But everybody says I am not the same boy that I used to be; and I know I am not. I love my poor sick mother, though; and I mean to help her all I can. This money will be of great use to her;" and Rufus looked with much satisfaction at the money which he held in his hand.

"I was almost afraid to pick berries to sell," he continued; "for I thought the boys would laugh at me; but I wanted very much to buy some tea for my mother, and so I resolved to try. Yesterday was the first day that I went into the fields; and when I saw you coming along the road, Willie, I wished I was at home again, for I could not bear to have you ridicule me. In trying to get out of your way, I spilled a part of my berries; and then you came to me *so kindly*, and offered to help me. Oh Willie! it did me good."

Here Rufus quite lost his self-control, and fairly sobbed aloud; and the tears rolled down Willie's cheeks also, though he felt very glad and thankful that he had been kind to the poor boy at a time when he so much needed kindness.

"I am *very, very* sorry that I ever laughed at

you," he again repeated. "Do not cry, Rufus, I will always love you."

"It is foolish in me to do so," said Rufus, struggling to be calm. "And I know it is wrong to mind being laughed at; but it is very hard to help it."

They had now reached the door of Mrs. Lyman's cottage; and Willie bade Rufus good-by, and walked thoughtfully toward home. He felt very desirous to help Rufus; but he did not see clearly what he could do for him.

"If I only had some money to buy him a new suit of clothes," he said to himself, "perhaps he would go to school again."

Willie's father and mother were not rich; and, as they had several children to provide for, Willie knew that it was not in their power to buy clothes for Rufus. He thought of his Uncle George, and wished he could ask him about it; but he had left home that morning, and would not return for several weeks.

After much reflection, Willie resolved that he would propose to Rufus to try to earn some money to buy clothes, and that he himself would help him all that he could in his play-hours.

Rufus received the proposition very gratefully. He felt very sure that he could earn clothes for himself, and money to buy various things for his mother besides, if Willie would help him. It was Willie's *sympathy*, more than his *assistance*, which Rufus needed. He was willing to work, now that he had a companion to encourage him and speak kindly to him.

The school-boys laughed when they saw Willie hard at work picking berries with the "Old Clothesman," as they called Rufus; but Willie took all their jokes good-naturedly, and Rufus soon learned to feel little disturbed by them.

Good berries found a ready sale; and, as Rufus was frequently employed by the neighboring farmers, who were glad to see that "the lad had taken the right start again," as they expressed it, there was soon money enough to purchase a neat suit of clothes; while Mrs. Lyman felt so comforted and cheered by the improvement in Rufus, that she was now gaining rapidly in health, and was able to do many things to aid in their support.

It was a happy day for Willie when Rufus, neatly dressed, and with a bright, happy countenance, once more entered the village school, and took his seat among the scholars. The teachers welcomed him cordially; and the boys, who had long since become ashamed of laughing at him, now gave him a cordial greeting.

As they were returning home that afternoon, a carriage, which was driving rapidly along the road in the same direction in which they were walking, suddenly stopped near Rufus and Willie, who were a little in advance of the other boys; and Willie, to his great delight, recognized his Uncle George, who had been absent for two months.

"Jump in, Willie," said Uncle George. "I am going to your father's, and will take you home."

"That is a bright-looking lad with whom you were walking," he continued, as they drove rapidly along. "Is he a school-mate of yours?"

"Why, uncle, that is Rufus Lyman!" exclaimed Willie. "Do not you remember seeing him the last time that we walked into the country together?"

"I remember poor Rufus very well," replied Uncle George; "but surely that was not he."

"It was indeed, uncle. He is a different boy now. I will tell you the whole story."

Uncle George listened with great interest to Willie's little tale.

"You have helped to do a good work, Willie," he said, when his nephew had finished. "Rufus will go on in the right path now, if I am not much mistaken. Was it not far better to give him a helping hand in this manner, than to push him along in the downward path?"

"Yes, indeed, uncle. I will never push any one down hill again. But I have not done much for Rufus; he has helped himself."

"Our Heavenly Father has helped you both, my boy. He has sent you to Rufus as a medium of His love; and He prepared the mind and heart of the poor fatherless boy to receive the good and truth thus offered him. Let us then bless His holy name, dear Willie; for it was indeed a good work."

CLARA'S BIRTHDAY;
OR,
THE MOTIVE MAKES THE DEED.

IT was a lovely morning in the month of June. The sun was shining brightly, and the gentle summer breeze scarcely misplaced Clara's clustering curls, as she threw open the window, that she might breathe the fragrance of the honeysuckle that grew so luxuriantly beneath it, and listen to the music of the birds, who were so joyously pouring forth their morning songs.

Clara felt unusually happy on this bright summer morning, for this was her tenth birthday, and she was joyfully anticipating the good wishes and pretty gifts which awaited her. Some months before, her father, who had noticed several faults in her character, which he wished to aid in correcting, had told her, after kindly pointing out the errors, that if he found that she had faithfully endeavored to remove them, he would give her as a reward, on her birthday, a beautiful workbox, such as Clara had long desired.

The little girl felt sure that she should receive the promised reward, for her weekly certificates from her teacher gave evidence of great improvement as a scholar, and her mother had frequently expressed her approbation at her newly-acquired habits of order and usefulness. So, as Clara stood by the open window enjoying the beautiful morning, she amused herself with various conjectures as to the appearance of the box, and the many pretty things it was to contain; and she was so busy with her own thoughts that she did not hear her father's step, nor think that he was near, until he placed a large paper parcel before her, and pleasantly wished her a happy birthday.

"Oh, father!" she exclaimed, joyfully. "Is this my work-box? I am so glad that you think I have improved. I was just thinking about my box, and wondering how it would look."

The string that tied the parcel was soon unfastened, and the work-box was found to equal Clara's highest expectations. She clapped her hands with delight when she saw its pretty lining of pink silk, and the bright silver thimble, and nice pair of scissors in a red morrocco case.

Her father was pleased with her joy, and he kissed her affectionately as he said, —

"I am very glad to make my Clara this birthday present, and I am glad to find that she is correcting some of her bad habits of idleness and disorder."

"Oh yes, father, I have tried very hard to do better. I always kept my pretty work-box in my mind, and whenever I felt tempted to be idle or careless, I would count the days that I had got to try for it, and that would help me to persevere. And now the happy day has come at last, and I have got my beautiful box;" and Clara danced around the room in her joy.

Her father smiled, but in a moment he looked grave and thoughtful, and, calling Clara to his side, he put his arm around her and said, —

"Do you know why I offered you this reward, my daughter?"

"I suppose you wanted to make me a better girl, father, and you thought this would be the best way to do it."

"Not exactly, Clara. I did not expect that trying for the work-box would make you really a better girl, but I thought that it might help you to correct some of your bad habits, and make it easier for you to be good at some future time."

"But shall I not be good, father, when I have corrected my faults?"

"You must learn to correct them from right motives, Clara. The hope of reward is a selfish motive. It is right to induce children and some other persons to do good from this motive, because it helps them to overcome evil habits; but I wish my little girl to remember that the motive makes the deed, and that no action is ever really good which is done from a selfish motive. Can you understand this hard lesson?"

"Oh yes, father, I understand what you mean, but it makes me very sorry, for I thought I had been such a good girl, and now I find that I have not."

"You need not be sorry, Clara. You have done very right in trying so perseveringly to conquer your faults from the motive which your father gave you; and your pretty box is a token of my approbation. But now that you are ten years old, it is time that you learned to examine your motives a little. I want you to think over what I have told you, and resolve to try from now till your next birthday to do right, not from the hope of reward, but because you love to obey the commandments of the Lord. This will be very hard at first. Even grown people find it difficult, and a great many do it very imperfectly, and some not at all; but I wish my little daughter to grow up to be a truly good woman, and therefore I am trying to teach her that the motive makes the deed."

"And I will try to remember it, father. It shall be my motto. And now may I go to my mother and show her my box, and tell her all that you have said to me?"

"All that you can remember, Clara. Your mother is not very well this morning, and will not leave her room."

Clara was grieved to hear this, for she was a very affectionate little girl, and she loved her parents dearly. She put both arms around her mother's neck and kissed her many times, and asked her if she had the headache, and what she could do to make her feel better.

Her mother told her that her head had ached badly all night, but she hoped it would soon be better, if she could be still a little while, and not be disturbed by the younger children; and Clara said she would be very kind to her little brothers and sisters, and would help to take care of the baby.

She showed her mother her birthday present, but did not then tell her what her father had said, because she knew that talking would make her head ache worse. She left the room softly, and went to the nursery, where she found Lizzie, the girl, dressing the children. They did not all look very pleasant, for they were accustomed to having their mother dress them, and were not willing to have Lizzie attend to them.

Henry, who was next to Clara in age, would not stand still to have his hair brushed; but when he saw his sister coming in, looking so neat and cheerful, he felt a little ashamed, and allowed the girl to smooth his curly locks. The little twins, Mary and Ellen, were both crying for mamma; but when sister Clara spoke kindly to them, and promised to show them her new box as soon as they were dressed, they dried their tears, and begged Lizzie to get them ready as soon as she could. Then dear little Willie, the youngest of all, crept up to Clara and hid his face in her dress, and when she took him in her arms and asked him how much he loved sister, he lisped " dee," which was his word for dearly, so sweetly, that it made her feel very happy, and she kissed him, and told him he was a darling baby.

After breakfast, as it was a fine morning, the children were all allowed to play in the yard and garden, and the house was so quiet that their mother got some rest; and about the middle of the forenoon she felt a little better, and was able to sit in the large rocking-chair, and the children were allowed to go into her room to see her. But her head still ached, and she could not bear much noise, so they did not stay long.

After Lizzie had taken the younger children away, Mrs. Merrill, Clara's mother, drew her little girl to her side, and took from the table a beautiful book of pictures and stories, which she told her was for a birthday gift.

Clara was much pleased, for she had not expected to receive any other present than the work-box. She kissed her mother, and thanked her, and then asked if she was now willing that she should go and invite several of her little friends in the neighborhood to come and pass the afternoon with her, as her mother had promised her she should do if the day was fine.

Mrs. Merrill hesitated. She did not love to disappoint Clara of this long-expected pleasure, but she was unwilling to have the little party on a day when she felt too ill to leave her room, for she always shared in the sports of her children, and knew very well that they would not be so good and happy without her. So, after a little thought, she told Clara that she should prefer not to have the party for another week.

The little girl looked very much disappointed, but she did not speak a word; and her mother, wishing to console her, told her that the strawberries would be ripe then, and the garden would look more beautiful with the bright flowers.

"Please, mother," said Clara, "do not tell me about those things. I want to be willing to give up the party from right motives; if I am only willing to give it up because it will be so much more pleasant in another week, those will be selfish motives."

Mrs. Merrill did not know of the conversation

which Clara had with her father in the morning, and she was quite surprised to hear her talking of the motives of her conduct.

Then Clara told her all that her father had said to her, and how she had resolved to try to do right from good motives.

"And so, mother," she said, "I am trying to be willing to give up my party because you are ill, and think it would be better for me to do so, and not because I shall have more pleasure another time."

"That is right, dear," said her mother; "and I am glad that my daughter is trying to keep so good a resolution. It is sometimes a difficult task to make our motives good; but if we ask the Lord to help us, the kind angels will come near, and teach us how to do right."

"But I cannot see the angels, mother."

"No, you cannot see them because your spiritual eyes are not opened; but when good thoughts and feelings come into your mind, and you desire to perform good actions, you may know that they are speaking to you, and trying to lead you in the right way. Always listen to them, dear Clara, and you will become more and more like them, until the Lord calls you to your heavenly home, and then you will also become an angel."

"I will try, dear mother," said Clara; and then she went softly from the room, and joined her little brothers and sisters, who were impatiently waiting for her.

The birthday passed happily away, and Clara's dreams that night were pleasant, for she had tried to do right.

And now that the new year had been so well begun, perhaps our little readers will think that it could not be very difficult to keep her resolution, and remember the motto that the "motive makes the deed." But Clara often found it very hard indeed; and if her kind father and mother had not watched over her and encouraged her, and taught her to feel that the angels were always ready to help her, she would have often been quite discouraged. But, as she persevered, her task gradually became more easy.

At first, she could not always tell whether her motives were good or evil, and would sometimes think she had done a very good action, when upon strict examination she would find that the motives were wrong.

"My Clara looks very bright and happy this morning," said Mrs. Merrill, as her daughter entered the room with her bonnet on, and her books under her arm, all ready for school.

"It is such a bright, pleasant morning, mother, that it makes me feel happy; and besides this, my own lessons are all well prepared, so that I shall have a great deal of time to help Addy; and this makes me glad, for I love to help her."

"Who is Addy, Clara? I think you have never told me about her."

"I thought I had told you, mother, but she has only been to our school for a few days. Her name is Adeline Morse. She is nearly as old as I am, but, until lately, her health has been very poor, so that she could not attend to her studies; and in many things she does not know as much as some of the youngest girls. Our teacher talked to us about her before she came, and told us that we must try to help her all we could, and be careful never to laugh at her ignorance. So we all promised to be kind to her; and indeed, mother, she is such a sweet little girl, that no one can help loving her. She is always so much pleased when she has learned anything new, and will kiss you and thank you so much for teaching her. She sits with me, so I show her more about her lessons than any one else, and I promised Miss Leslie to study hard myself, and learn some lessons at home, so that I might have time. She said I was a very good girl to love to help Addy."

"It is very kind in you, certainly, Clara, but you must be careful not to forget your motto."

"'The motive makes the deed!' No, mother, I will not forget it; but you know my motive in teaching Addy must be good. I do not receive any reward for doing it."

"Not exactly, Clara, and yet I think I can see that selfishness might become mixed with your love of being useful to her. Guard your heart carefully, my daughter. And now kiss me, and I will bid you good-morning, for it is time you were on your way."

"I will walk fast, mother, for I have received no mark for tardiness this term."

And with an affectionate good-morning, Clara was soon walking rapidly toward the school-house.

Very truly had Clara said that Adeline was a "sweet little girl." She came forward to meet her new friend with such a glad, loving smile, and twined her arms around her neck so gently, as she whispered, "I am so glad you have come, dear Clara; my lesson in arithmetic is very difficult this morning, and now you will explain it all to me. The other girls would have shown me, but I would rather wait for you."

Clara's bright face grew brighter still, as she heard these words. It was very pleasant to be looked up to, and to feel that Adeline loved her, and valued her assistance so highly.

"I will show you in one moment, dear Addy," she replied, "just as soon as I have hung up my bonnet."

Clara was an excellent scholar for her age, and what had appeared difficult to Adeline seemed very plain to her, and she soon succeeded in making it equally so to her little companion. Both were pleased and happy, and the teacher bestowed praises upon both when the well-learned lesson was recited.

For several weeks Clara continued to render daily assistance to her friend, and Adeline made great improvement under her tuition. Nothing gave Clara more pleasure than to hear the praises which were frequently bestowed upon her little pupil, and she often learned her own lessons in play-hours, that she might have more leisure to attend to Adeline.

One morning she was unavoidably detained at home until a late hour. Her mother gave her a written excuse for her teacher, and as soon as she had handed it to her, she took her seat. It was nearly time for Adeline's class to recite in arithmetic, and the little girl was very busily engaged with a long sum.

"I will show you now, Addy," whispered Clara. "I could not come before."

"Please, Clara, do not speak to me for one minute," was the reply. "I do believe I shall get it right myself, and I have tried so long."

Clara turned away to attend to her own lessons. There was no reason for her feeling hurt or out of humor. Adeline had spoken very gently, and it was certainly right for her to wish to do the sum without assistance, if she could. Why, then, did Clara feel unkindly; and why, when the slate was handed to the teacher, and the answer pronounced correct, did she turn coldly away from the sparkling glance which her friend directed toward her, as if for sympathy in her joy?

"Are you sick, dear Clara?" asked Adeline, as she again took her seat at her side.

"Not at all," she replied, "but I must study my lessons. It is very late."

"Then I will try not to disturb you with questions. Perhaps I can find all those places upon the map myself. There is nothing like trying. I thought I should never do that long sum, but it was right at last."

Intent upon her own lesson, and desirous not to disturb her friend, Adeline did not, for some time, discover Clara's ill-humor. At length, however, after a long search for one of the many places which she was to find upon the map, she turned to her for assistance.

"Just this one place, if you please, Clara; I will try not to interrupt you again."

"There is nothing like trying," replied Clara shortly. "You had better find it yourself."

Adeline looked with a surprised and mournful expression in Clara's face.

"Have I done anything to offend you, Clara?" she asked, gently.

"Oh, no," was the reply, "but it is better for you to depend upon yourself."

With tears in her eyes, Adeline returned to her task. The place was found at length, but she was still very sad, for the ill-humor of her friend appeared to her unaccountable.

In vain she endeavored to find out the cause: Clara would give no explanation;—indeed, she continued to say that nothing was the matter, but it was quite evident that this was untrue.

When school was dismissed, instead of walking along arm-in-arm as usual, the two little girls rather seemed to avoid each other, and went home by different paths.

Everything seemed to go wrong with Clara. She had listened to the voice of the evil spirits, and the good angels were not near her now. Every duty seemed irksome, and was unwillingly performed. Toward evening, her mother requested her to take charge of the baby for an hour, as the girl had gone out, and she herself was busily engaged with some sewing.

Clara made no objection, but was so careless and inattentive to the little boy's wants, that he soon wearied of her care.

"I cannot keep him quiet, mother," said Clara,

in answer to a remonstrance from her mother. "I am sure I have tried my best."

"Your heart is not in it, Clara," was the reply, "and therefore you do not succeed. I am sorry on your own account; for, if I am obliged to leave my work, I shall not be able to complete your new frock in season for you to wear it to the little party to which you are invited to-morrow."

Clara had not thought of this. She was very desirous to wear her new frock to the party.

"Stop one minute, mother," she said; "please do not take Willie yet, and I will get my doll for him. That always makes him stop crying."

Clara's heart was in it now, and the baby was soon contented and happy.

When it was nearly dusk, and Mrs. Merrill laid aside her work and was ready to take him, Clara looked triumphantly at the clock, as she said,—

"I have kept Willie happy for an hour and a half, mother. Is not that doing pretty well?"

"The *deed* was good, certainly, Clara, if the *motive* was an unselfish one."

Clara made no reply. This was the first time she had thought of her motto through the day. She appeared to be thinking deeply, and her mother did not disturb her, but left the room to put the baby to bed.

"The motive makes the deed," repeated Clara to herself, when she was left alone. "No wonder father told me that it was difficult to remember this. I did not care anything about pleasing Willie until I found that if I did not, I could not have my new dress to wear to-morrow. That was a selfish motive, and I believe I have been selfish all the afternoon. Everything has seemed to go wrong."

Clara was a little girl, but she had been taught to examine herself, and her thoughts now went back to the school-room, and she continued her examination.

"I was cross this morning, also," she said. "Poor Addy! I wonder what made me treat her so unkindly. I have always loved to help her before. Somehow it made me cross when I found that she had learned her arithmetic lesson without me, but I do not know why it should;—I ought to have been glad. There is father walking in the garden; I will go and tell him all about it, and he will help me to see how I have done wrong."

Clara's Birthday.

This was a very wise resolution. Children should always recollect that their parents are their best advisers. They should never conceal their faults from them, but frankly tell all their thoughts and feelings, and be guided by their advice.

Mr. Merrill listened very kindly to Clara's little story. He was very glad to find that she was learning to examine the motives of her actions, and he could see very plainly why she had felt disturbed and vexed at finding that Adeline could learn a lesson without her assistance.

"We are often mistaken in our motives, dear Clara," he said, "and it sometimes takes some severe lessons to help us to understand them. I suppose you have always thought, that in assisting your little friend, you were trying only to do her good."

"Yes, father, I did not receive any reward for teaching her."

"Did not your teacher frequently praise you for your kindness, Clara; and did not Adeline herself show you much gratitude and love on this account?"

"Yes, father, but I do not think I did it for the sake of receiving their praise."

"Not wholly, Clara, but this must have been partly your motive. If you had felt no desire for any reward excepting the pleasure of seeing Adeline improve, you would not have felt displeased when you found that she was learning to do without your assistance. On the contrary, you would have felt pleased and happy. The little occurrence of this morning shows you that your motives were not entirely unselfish. You thought more of the praise which you received, and of the gratitude which Adeline showed you, than you did of the good which you were doing."

Clara was quite silent for some minutes, and then she said,—

"I think you are right, father. I can see now that my motives were not wholly good. But indeed I thought they were. It seemed to me that I could never be tired of teaching Adeline. I loved to do it so much, and I thought it was such a good thing to do. I am afraid I shall never be good, father."

"You must not be discouraged, Clara. I have no doubt that you have done Adeline a great deal of good, and from right motives, too. A little selfishness has crept in, but now you have discovered it, you will try to put it away."

"Yes, father, and I will ask my Heavenly Father to help me; and now I will go and tell mother all about it, and ask her to forgive me for having been so cross this afternoon. Everything went wrong after I was unkind to Adeline."

"Evil spirits were near you, my daughter. Little by little you will learn to guard your heart from them."

Very earnestly did Clara try to keep the angels near to her. She and Adeline soon became warmer friends than ever before, but there was less selfishness mingled with their love. Clara was still ever ready to assist her friend in her studies when it was really necessary, but she also seemed most happy when she could accomplish the task by her own perseverance; and Adeline, although less dependent upon Clara, found great encouragement and pleasure in her kindness and sympathy.

New trials were continually arising, and it was still difficult to keep the motto in mind. It was easier to do right in great things than in little ones, Clara often said, and this is very true. A great many grown people, as well as children, find it easier to do right when some very important duty is to be performed, than to do good continually in trifling, every-day duties.

Often, when playing with her brothers and sisters, or her young companions, Clara would find herself in danger of being selfish; and often, also, when she had done what seemed to be right, she would discover that the motive which prompted the action was not what it ought to have been; but still she persevered, and gradually she learned to examine her motives before she commenced any new undertaking.

Her mother had taken into the family a little colored girl, whom she intended to educate and bring up, to assist her in the house. The child was very ignorant, and Mrs. Merrill proposed to Clara that she should teach her to read.

Clara was delighted, and for some days could think of nothing else. Every leisure moment was devoted to her new pupil, but the child was inattentive and dull, and she soon wearied of her task, and, before long, entirely neglected it.

"Has Annie learned all her letters yet?" asked

Mr. Merrill, as he saw the little girl with a book in her hand one morning.

"I believe not, father,—I am not sure. It is some time since I have heard her read," replied Clara, blushing.

"But I thought you had taken charge of that branch of her education, Clara."

"So I did, father; but she is so idle and dull, that there is no pleasure in teaching her."

"Was pleasure your *motive* in undertaking to teach her, Clara?"

Clara blushed again as she answered,—

"I am afraid it was partly my motive, father. I thought it would be a very easy task, and that I should enjoy doing it, but I was mistaken."

"Supposing you try again from different motives, Clara; I think you would succeed."

Clara thought for a little while. She did not feel very willing to do what her father proposed, and yet she knew that it would be doing right. She did not answer hastily, therefore, but after considering a little, she said earnestly,—

"I will try to do it from good motives, father."

"That is all I wish you to do, my child; and if you try, I feel sure you will succeed."

Three months after this conversation, little Annie could read fluently in easy reading, and her young teacher said that she had become so industrious, and easy to learn, that it was a pleasure to teach her.

"So you have the *pleasure* after all, Clara," observed her father, smilingly, as he heard this remark.

"Yes, father, but that is not the reason that I teach her."

"I know it, my daughter, and it makes me very happy to think that you are beginning to find pleasure in the faithful performance of duty. This is the only true happiness."

The year passed swiftly away, and again it was Clara's birthday. She was not now anticipating any beautiful gift as a reward for her improvement, but this did not prevent her from feeling very happy. Indeed, it seemed to her that this was the happiest, most lovely birthday she had ever known. Again she sat by the open window, and, as she breathed the fragrance of the honeysuckle, listened to the music of the birds, and rejoiced in the bright sunshine, her little heart seemed filled with love and gratitude to her Heavenly Father, who, during the past year, had enabled her to shun many evil ways, and to love to keep His commandments more than she had ever done before.

While she was thinking of these things, her father's kind voice was heard at the door bidding her good-morning, and she hastened to open it, and to tell him how happy she felt on this beautiful birthday morning.

"I am glad you are happy, my daughter, and here is a birthday gift from your mother and myself;" and, as he spoke, he handed a very small package to Clara.

She opened it, and, to her surprise and joy, found a beautiful ring, with a bright red stone in it, just such as she had often wished for.

"Oh, thank you, father!" she exclaimed; "I never had a ring before in all my life. Only look! it fits me exactly, and it is so bright and pretty."

"This ring has another virtue besides its beauty," said Mr. Merrill, smiling at her joy. "Look in the inside."

Clara looked, and found these words neatly engraven: "The motive makes the deed."

HENRY'S NAP IN THE ARBOR.

"I AM so glad there is no school this afternoon," said little Henry Warren, "for now I can read the new book that Aunt Martha sent me. And after I have read it, mother," he continued, "may I lend it to Johnny Roper? for you know he is sick, and cannot go out to play, and he likes to read very much."

"Yes, you may lend it to him," replied Mrs. Warren; "and I am glad that you wish to do so. I love to have you kind and thoughtful."

"I should not like to be selfish, mother," said Henry; "Georgie Blake has got a new book, and Johnny's sister asked him if he would lend it to her for Johnny to read; but he would not let her take it. He only said that he did not like to lend his books; he was afraid they would get spoiled."

"That was not very kind, certainly," answered his mother; "but perhaps you do selfish things sometimes, Henry, though not exactly of the same kind."

"No, mother, I do not think I am selfish," replied Henry, looking very earnestly in his mother's face. "I always lend my books and toys, and, very often, when I have candy or fruit, I give a part of it away. I gave Sam Gordon half of the pear that you gave me this morning."

"But there are a great many ways of being selfish, besides being unwilling to give away or lend our things, Henry," said his mother, smiling a little at his earnestness; "but we will not talk about them now, as you are in haste to read your new book. I have looked it over, and I think you will find it very interesting."

"I think so too, mother, for Aunt Martha always sends me *very* interesting books. I will sit in my favorite seat by the window in the sitting-room."

Henry ran for his book, and was soon seated by the window, reading away very busily. He had been engaged in this way about half an hour, when he heard footsteps in the yard; and, peeping through the closed blind, he saw two boys, considerably younger than himself, walking along the path which led to the house.

"Oh dear!" said Henry to himself, "if there isn't Charlie and Willie Lewis. I do wish they had stayed at home. I don't want to play with them one bit. I will go and tell mother."

So saying, Henry rose from his seat, and went to the room where Mrs. Warren was busy with her sewing.

"Mother," said he, as he opened the door, "Charlie and Willie Lewis are coming up the yard. I suppose they have come to play with me, but I want to read very much; and, besides, they are such little fellows, there is no fun in playing with them. Could you please send them home, mother?"

"Why, Henry, that would be very rude and unkind. What could I say to them?"

"Tell them that you want me this afternoon, can't you, mother? You know you do want me to read my book."

Mrs. Warren shook her head. "No, no, Henry," she said, "that would not be strictly true; and, besides that, it would be selfish to send the children home, merely because you wish to read. You do not wish to be selfish, you know. Hark! they are knocking. Go and open the door with a pleasant face, my son, and give your little friends a cordial welcome. You will enjoy your book all the more another time."

Thus urged, Henry went to the door, but he did it slowly and reluctantly; and, if the little boys had looked in his face when he asked them to walk in, they would certainly have seen that he was not very glad to see them.

But they felt a little shy and awkward at coming to a new place, so they kept their eyes fixed on the floor, and only said, "Yes, ma'am," and "No, ma'am," when Henry's mother asked them any questions. The weather was very fine, and Mrs. Warren presently advised Henry to take his little friends into the yards and garden. She knew they would feel more at home out of doors, and she hoped that Henry would forget his disappointment, and try to make their visit pleasant to them.

But Henry was not only vexed that his reading was interrupted, but he was also a little displeased that Charlie and Willie should have come to visit him. Like many other boys of nine or ten, he felt himself altogether too large to play with those who were two or three years younger. He walked around the garden with his little visitors, and showed them his pet rabbits and his chickens, but he did not propose any play, or make any great effort to amuse them. By and by his mother came to the door, and gave each of the boys a cake and an apple, and advised them to have a game of hide and seek.

"Charlie and Willie will enjoy it, I think," she said to Henry, "and you can find a great many good places to hide in, around the yards and in the barn."

Henry still looked very sober, but he made no objection; and, as soon as they had finished eating, they began the game. Charlie and Willie could play this very well. Each took his turn in hiding, and then came Henry's turn. As he passed around the house on his way to the barn, where he intended hiding, he caught a glimpse of his new book through the half-open blinds of the sitting-room. It was lying on the table just where he had left it.

"Oh, there is my new book," he said to himself.

"How I do wish I could read in it, just for a little while. I mean to put my hand through the blind and get it, and hide in the summer-house at the foot of the garden. The boys will not find me there very soon, and I shall have a nice time reading."

So Henry pushed the blind open a little further, and took the book from the table, and buttoned it under his jacket. He then went into the barn for a moment, and called "whoop," loudly. He knew that the boys would listen for this call, and be guided by the sound of his voice. He did not remember that it would be wrong to deceive them, and make them think that he was in the barn, when he had no intention of hiding there. The moment that he had called "whoop," he crept softly out of a back door; and, being very careful not to go in the direction where the boys were, he ran quickly into the garden, and in a few minutes reached the little summer-house. It was a very pleasant, shady place, and Henry seated himself with great satisfaction, and opened his book. He read one chapter with much pleasure; but then he began to feel a little uneasy as he thought of Charlie and Willie.

"They must have searched the barn all over by this time," he said to himself. "I wonder where they will look next. I don't believe they will think of this place. Perhaps they will give up, and go home. I wish they would; but then mother will say I was rude. I have a great mind to stop reading, and go back to them; but it is so stupid playing with such little fellows. I don't see what they came here for."

So Henry read another chapter, and by that time he had grown still more uneasy, but now he felt ashamed to go back to the boys, and concluded to wait until he felt pretty sure that they had gone home.

"I do not think they will go into the house," he said, "and mother will know nothing about it."

But still Henry did not feel easy. His conscience told him that he had done wrong. He no longer felt any interest in reading, but sat quite still, listening for the footsteps of the boys, and thinking what his mother would say if she *should* find out what he had done. Pretty soon he fell fast asleep, with one hand still tightly clasping his new book, while the other rested on the arm of the little settee which formed the seat of the arbor.

Charlie and Willie meanwhile having searched the barn and other outbuildings in vain, concluded that Henry must have gone into the house; and as they felt unwilling to go in to look for him, they resolved to sit down under the trees and wait until he came out; but, after waiting a long time, they grew impatient and tired, and thought they would go home.

"I don't believe he means to come out again," said Charlie; "I guess his mother wants him."

"He ought to come and tell us so," replied Willie. "I do not think he is at all polite."

So the two little boys went home, feeling rather unkindly toward Henry. Mrs. Warren being busy with her work in the house, knew nothing of what was passing.

A little before five o'clock, Henry's uncle drove to the door with his horse and chaise, and asked if Henry was at home.

"Yes," replied his mother, "he is round the house, somewhere; he has company this afternoon."

"Oh, he has company!" repeated his uncle.

"Never mind, then; I was thinking of inviting him to take a ride. I have business about five miles from here, and I thought he would like to go with me."

"He would like it very much, I am sure," replied Mrs. Warren; "and, as the little boys were to go home at five, I will call him, and let him go, if you can wait a moment."

"Please do it as quickly as possible," returned her brother, "for it is growing late, and I am in haste."

Mrs. Warren ran to the barn, and called loudly for Henry, but there was no answer. She then went into the back yard, but he was not there. She opened the garden gate also, and looked in and called once or twice, but the summer-house was at the most distant part of the garden, and Henry was sleeping too soundly to be easily aroused. Quite disappointed, she returned to her brother.

"I cannot find him," she said, "and I will not detain you any longer. He has probably walked part of the way home with the little boys who have been visiting him."

"Very likely," was the reply; and in another

moment the chaise was wheeling rapidly out of sight.

"I am really sorry that Henry could not have gone," said Mrs. Warren to herself, as she walked into the house; "it would have given him so much pleasure. I wonder that he did not bring the little boys into the house to bid me good-by before they went home."

Soon after this, Mrs. Warren took a small dish in her hand, and went into the garden to gather some fruit for tea. There were some fine blackberries growing in the lower part of the garden, and she had noticed in the morning that they were quite ripe. She soon filled her dish, and, in returning to the house, she happened to take a path which led directly by the summer-house, or arbor. She was very much surprised, as you may suppose, when she saw Henry sitting there, fast asleep.

She put her hand on his shoulder, and shook him a little, and spoke to him gently, and pretty soon he opened his eyes.

At first he looked about him, quite bewildered, but in a minute or two he remembered all that had passed.

"Where are Charlie and Willie, mother?" he asked, looking earnestly in his mother's face.

"I do not know, Henry; I supposed you were with them. It is after five now. How long have you been sleeping here?"

"After five, mother!" exclaimed Henry, in astonishment. "Why! it was only three when I came here."

"And why did you come here, Henry? Where did you leave the little boys?"

Henry hung his head and looked ashamed, as he heard his mother's questions.

"Tell me the whole truth, my boy," continued his mother. "I presume you have done wrong, or your new book would not be in your hands. The best thing you can do now, is to be perfectly honest in confessing your fault."

So Henry told his mother the whole story, and did not try to excuse himself at all.

"I know that it was wrong, mother," he said, "and I am very sorry. I see now that I am selfish in some ways, although I *am* willing to lend my books and toys. If you will please to tell Charlie and Willie's mother all about it, and ask her to let them come again, I will try to make them very happy."

"I am glad that you are willing to do right about it, Henry, and I will think what had better be done. I suppose the little boys have gone home, for I have looked in the barn, and in several other places, and they were not there. Your uncle came to ask you to take a ride with him, a little before five, and as it was so nearly time for the boys to go, I thought it would not be wrong for you to leave them, but I could not find you, and your uncle was in haste."

Henry felt very much disappointed when he heard of the pleasant ride he had lost, and his eyes filled with tears, but he did not say a word, for he knew that it was his own fault.

His mother felt sorry for him, and talked kindly to him as they walked together to the house. She saw that he felt grieved and ashamed at what had happened, and she was careful not to add to his trouble by any reproaches. A few days after this, she called upon Mrs. Lewis, and told her the whole story, and begged her to allow Charlie and Willie to pass another afternoon with

Henry, and Mrs. Lewis readily consented that they should do so.

This second visit was a very happy one to all parties, for Henry was very careful not to think of his own pleasure, but to do everything in his power to entertain his little visitors; and they were so pleased with his kindness, that they told their mother, when they returned home, that they had never passed such a delightful afternoon.

MISCHIEVOUS TOM;

OR,

IT IS ONLY FOR FUN.

TOM STEVENS was an intelligent and good-tempered boy, and was generally a favorite with his friends and companions, on account of his pleasant, obliging disposition. No one would have thought of accusing Tom of selfishness, for he was always ready to share what he had with others, and would frequently give away even more than he kept for himself.

Tom's greatest fault seemed to be too strong a love for what he called *fun;* and, in pursuing his sports, he was not always careful to regard the feelings and comfort of those around him. When a very little boy, he would snatch away the rattle from his baby-brother, and hold it behind him; and, when the infant cried and held out his little hands, Tom would laugh loudly as he handed it to him, and exclaim, "Oh, what good fun!" If the dog and cat were quietly eating their breakfast, he would brandish a stick over their heads, and frighten them away; and nothing pleased him more than to jump out suddenly from behind a door when some one was passing through, and thus startle and frighten him.

Tom's parents and other friends often talked with him concerning this fault, and tried to convince him how wrong it was. They told him that it was one of the worst kinds of selfishness to find pleasure in giving pain to others; but Tom, although he did not like to be called selfish, took no pains to reform; and, even after he became a large boy, would often indulge in these selfish sports.

His sister Mary had a beautiful canary-bird, which Tom had himself given her for a birthday present. He had saved his pocket-money for a long time to enable him to do this kindness to his sister; and no one would have supposed, that, after this self-denial had put it in his power to give her so much pleasure, he would have taken any satisfaction in teasing and vexing her about the bird.

But it happened that a gentleman, at whose

house he was visiting, made Tom a present of a stuffed canary-bird, exactly resembling Mary's sweet little songster. It immediately occurred to him, that this would be a fine opportunity to play a trick upon Mary. He knew that she always visited her bird the first thing in the morning; and, rising very early, he secretly took the living bird from the cage, and put the stuffed one in its place. He contrived to place it upon the perch in such a way that it looked as if it were alive; and then, carrying the real bird to his own room, secured him carefully in an old cage which he had there.

When little Mary came down stairs, she hastened, as usual, to feed her favorite, and clean his pretty house. She was much surprised that he did not begin to chirp and flutter as usual at her approach; and she said sorrowfully to her mother, who had just entered the room, that she feared poor birdy was sick. She took down the cage; and, opening the door, held a lump of sugar to his bill to see if he would eat; but, the moment she touched him, he fell from the perch; and, taking him up, she found he was quite cold and lifeless. Bursting into tears, she ran to her mother, and hid her face in her lap, sobbing out, "O mother, mother! my sweet pet is dead!"

Just then Tom sprang from his hiding-place, where he had been watching the whole scene, exclaiming, —

"No, no, Mary! he is not dead. That is not your bird at all. I have him safe in my cage upstairs. This is a stuffed one which Mr. Watson gave me. But wasn't it good fun to see you hold the sugar to his bill?" And at this recollection, Tom rolled on the floor, almost convulsed with laughter.

"It may be 'good fun' to you, Tom," replied his mother, gravely; "but it was great pain to your sister, and I think it a wicked and foolish joke. Some day, my son, I fear you will learn from bitter experience that there is little fun in selfish sport. Mischief, sooner or later, will bring just punishment upon its author."

Merry Tom was not convinced by what his mother said. He, however, ran gayly up-stairs, and soon returned with poor Mary's bird, who had been much surprised at his change of residence. Mary was too much delighted to have her little pet, again to think of reproaching her brother, and was soon busily engaged in giving him his morning meal.

That same day, as Tom was returning from school, he stopped for a few moments at old Susan's cottage. Susan had formerly lived with Tom's mother; and the children were fond of her, and often visited her, and carried with them little presents which their mother gave them for the purpose. Tom, in particular, was a great favorite with Susan; and, indeed, he was very kind to her. She lived alone with an orphan niece, — a little girl about the age of Mary, — and was often glad of his assistance in various ways. In the winter, when the snow was deep, he was careful to shovel good paths around her house, and to see that she was well supplied with wood and water; and, in the spring and summer, he spent many a play-hour in her little garden, assisting in the cultivation of the various vegetables with which the plot of ground was well filled.

On the morning of which we are speaking, Tom observed that the little peach-tree, which both he and Susan had watched over so carefully, was quite full of peaches, and that they appeared to be very nearly ripe.

"You will have a fine basket of peaches from your little tree, Susan," he said, as he entered the cottage. "When do you mean to gather them?"

"To-morrow morning, Master Tom; and, if you will call in on your way to school, you shall have a dozen of the best that are gathered. Many a night I have lain awake, thinking of my little peach-tree, and hoping that the naughty boys in the neighborhood would not rob me of its fruit; but I believe they have too much good feeling to wish to trouble a poor old woman like myself. At any rate, I am pretty safe from them now; for, in twenty-four hours more, the peaches will be picked, and in a safe place."

"I will not forget to call for my share," said Tom, laughing, as he bade the good woman good-morning, and advised her still to keep a sharp watch for the thieves, for they might come at the last moment.

As he walked along to school, he thought what a fine plan it would be to go himself and gather the peaches that evening, and hide them in some safe place until the next day.

"It would be such fun," he said to himself, "to see poor Susan's consternation, when she finds her tree empty! And, after all, I should be doing her a service; for it would save her the trouble of gathering the peaches herself." He knew that she went to bed very early, and that there would be little danger of his being discovered if he went any time after dark.

So, after tea that evening, Tom told his parents that he was going to play for a little while; and they, charging him to be home in good season, and not to get into any mischief, readily gave their consent.

He secretly took a large basket with him, which he hid near Susan's cottage; and then, joining some of his companions, played merrily until the time arrived when he thought it would be safe to put his plan into execution. Between eight and nine o'clock, he softly opened the gate of the little garden, and, standing beneath the peach-tree, looked carefully around. All was still.

"Susan has gone to bed long ago," said he. "Now I will make quick work of it." And, in another moment, he was busily engaged in putting the peaches into the basket.

Now, it happened that a neighboring farmer had called in to see Susan that evening concerning some spinning which his wife wished to have done; and, finding her rather lonely, had sat for an hour or two to enjoy a little social chat. As they were on the back side of the house, and Tom was on the front, he did not perceive that the lamp was still burning, or he would have known at once that it was not safe to play his intended trick. The farmer's dog lay on the doorstep, enjoying a comfortable nap; but, being disturbed by some slight sound, he started up with a quick bark, and, seeing Tom at the peach-tree, ran forward, and seized him by the leg. In vain poor Tom struggled to get free; the dog held him fast; and, in another moment, the farmer rushed from the cottage, and calling to Susan to stay within, lest she should get the rheumatism from exposure to the night air, he caught hold of the collar of the supposed thief, and, with a stout cane which he held in his hand, gave him a most severe beating.

Smarting with bodily pain, and overwhelmed with mortification, Tom would gladly have retreated in silence; but after the farmer had punished him, as he thought, sufficiently, he dragged him toward the cottage, exclaiming,—

"Now come to the light, my boy, and let us see who you are, that would rob a poor woman of her little store."

Escape was impossible. Susan came eagerly forward with a blazing lamp, the light from which no sooner fell upon the countenance of the prisoner, than she exclaimed in astonishment,—

"Master Tom! Can it be possible? Surely, Farmer Roberts, there must be some mistake. This is not the boy who was stealing my peaches."

"The very same, ma'am. There stands his basket with some of the fruit already in it; but, thanks to my good dog, he had no time to escape with his booty. And now I suppose he will not turn thief again in a hurry, for my oaken stick has become pretty well acquainted with his back."

"I was not going to steal your peaches, Susan," said Tom, struggling for utterance. "I only meant to hide them until morning, just to play you a little trick."

Susan was so much shocked and grieved at what had taken place, that it was some time before she could understand the truth of the matter. When the whole story was explained,

Farmer Roberts expressed his regret for the severe punishment which he had given Tom.

"But it may be a useful lesson to you, my boy," he said kindly. "Those who indulge in mischief at the expense of the feelings of others, are generally punished in one way or another."

Tom now took his basket, and crept toward home, rather discontented with the result of his evening's sport. Although very sore and lame from the effects of the beating, he tried to appear as usual before his parents, hoping that the affair might be kept secret; but, very early the next morning, Susan was at the house to inquire how he was, and to beg Mrs. Stevens to forgive her for what had occurred.

Neither Mr. nor Mrs. Stevens regretted the lesson which Tom had received. They hoped it would have a salutary effect, and kindly comforted Susan, assuring her that she was not at all to blame. The story soon got abroad in the village, and was considered an excellent joke among Tom's school-fellows.

But one lesson, however severe, was not enough to cure him of his inveterate love for selfish sports, or "good fun," as he denominated it.

Not very long after the affair of the peach-tree, Tom was one day amusing himself with sailing about a small pond in the garden, in a little boat which his father kept for the purpose. Tom had been taught to row, and there was little danger of any accident, if he was cautious. Presently he saw his sister Mary standing near the edge of the pond, looking earnestly at him.

"Would you like to have a sail, Mary?" he asked good-naturedly, at the same time rowing toward the spot where she stood.

"Very much," replied Mary, "if you think mother would be willing to trust me with you."

"To be sure she would," answered her brother. "Father says I can manage this boat as well as he can. Give me your hand, and I will help you in."

Mary enjoyed her sail exceedingly, and soon felt quite at her ease. For some time all went well; but, at last, Tom could not resist his inclination to play her a little trick. Seizing an opportunity when she was not observing him, he threw a little water into the bottom of the boat, and then suddenly exclaimed, as if in much affright, —

"O Mary! what shall we do? The boat has

sprung a leak, and will certainly go to the bottom! See, see! She is filling with water already!"

Mary uttered a loud scream, and, before Tom could detain her, sprung from her seat so hastily, that she lost her balance, and fell into the water. It was in the very middle of the pond; and she must soon have been drowned, had not the gardener, alarmed by her cries, rushed to her assistance. He swam toward the spot where she had sunk, and, with some difficulty, succeeded in raising her, and carrying her to the shore. She was quite insensible, and for some time her anxious parents, and the physician who had been called, hung over her, uncertain whether she would ever breathe again.

Tom was overcome with horror and remorse at the sad consequences of his silly trick; but when his sister revived, and, after a few days, was nearly as well as usual, the remembrance of his grief faded from his mind, and he was soon as fond of mischief as ever.

There was an old colored man, who had long been employed by Tom's father, and was held in high esteem by all the family. Paul, — for so he was called, — was naturally rather timid; and was, in particular, a strong believer in all the foolish tales of departed spirits. One day, when walking with Tom in a lonely place at some distance from the house, he pointed to a large tree, saying, with a sort of shudder, —

"That is the haunted tree, Master Tom. Many years ago, an unfortunate man, who was supposed to have committed some fearful crime which had escaped detection, hung himself upon a bough of that tree. Ever since that time, if you pass the place after nightfall, strange sounds are heard among the branches, resembling the groans of a dying man."

Tom laughed heartily at this idle tale, and assured Paul that he would take the first opportunity of visiting the place after dark, that he might himself hear these strange sounds, and judge what they meant. Paul solemnly warned him against the indulgence of such foolish curiosity, and the conversation was dropped.

Not many evenings after, Paul was sent of an errand to a neighboring village. It was necessary for him to pass the dreaded tree, and Tom shook his head at him as he went out, saying, —

"Beware of the ghost, Paul!"

The poor old man mustered up all his courage, and walked steadily and safely by the spot; then, rejoicing in his success, he went happily on his way. It was darker when he returned, and his fears increased as he drew near the tree; but, remembering that all was silent when he passed it before, he walked swiftly along. Immediately, however, he heard the most fearful groans from among the branches, accompanied by other sounds, that seemed most horrible to poor frightened Paul. At first, he was so overcome with terror, that he stood quite motionless, and seemed about to sink to the ground; but, recovering himself a little, he took to his heels, and ran for dear life. Directly the air resounded with merry Tom's shouts of langhter; and, looking back, Paul saw his young master perched among the highest branches of the haunted tree. Relieved of his fears, but at the same time vexed at the trick which had been played him, he slowly returned, calling to Tom to mind how he came down; for the tree was a difficult one to climb, and, if he did not stop laughing, he would be very likely to miss his foot-hold.

"O Paul, Paul, how funny you looked!" exclaimed Tom, redoubling his merriment at the thought. It would have been far better had he regarded Paul's warning; for, at this moment, his foot slipped,—a small branch of which he had hold gave way,—and he fell to the ground.

Paul hastened to assist him; but he soon found that some sad accident must have taken place in the fall, for Tom could not rise without screaming with pain. He was carried home, and a physician called, who told them that he had broken his right leg badly, and it would be many weeks before he could use it at all.

This was, indeed, a severe punishment. For a long time Tom was confined to one position, and entirely unable to join in the sports of his companions. Besides this, he suffered a great deal of pain, and it was feared that he would be always lame.

Now he had leisure to reflect upon the causes of this sad disaster; and, for the first time in his life, he saw his conduct in its true light, and truly repented of the selfish pleasure which he had found in giving pain to others.

In after-life he carefully avoided every kind of selfish sport; and, whenever he met with those who took delight in this species of " good fun," he would tell them his own history, and assure them that mischief will, sooner or later, bring evil consequences upon its author.

www.ingramcontent.com/pod-product-compliance
Lightning Source LLC
Chambersburg PA
CBHW020845160426
43192CB00007B/791